HAVE RACQUET • WILL TRAVEL

HAVE RACQUET · WILL TRAVEL
WILLIAM EMRICH

Haley's
Athol, Massachusetts

Copyright 2018 by William Emrich.

All rights reserved. With the exception of short excerpts in a review or critical article, no part of this book may be re-produced by any means, including information storage and retrieval or photocopying equipment, without written permission of the publisher, Haley's.

Haley's
488 South Main Street
Athol, MA 01331
haley.antique@verizon.net
800.215.8805

Photos and mementos from the author's collection.

To protect the identity of some individuals, the author has changed their names in the following account,

Library of Congress CataloginginPublication Data
Names: Emrich, William, author.
Title: Have racquet will travel / William Emrich.
Description: Athol, MA : Haley's, [2018]
Identifiers: LCCN 2017051035 | ISBN 9780996773058 (trade pbk.) Subjects: LCSH: Emrich, WilliamTravel. | Tennis playersUnited StatesBiography.
Classification: LCC GV994.E67 A3 2018 | DDC 796.342092 [B] dc23 LC record available at https://lccn.loc.gov/2017051035

To my father,
for whom I will always have
tremendous love and respect, and
to whom I owe so much

You will make all kinds of mistakes;
but as long as you are generous and true, and also fierce,
you cannot hurt the world or
even seriously distress her.
She was made to be wooed and
won by youth.
—Sir Winston Churchill
Roving Commission: My Early Life

Contents

Photos and Mementos xi

A Prophetic Surprise Presentation 1

At Home on the Courts from an Early Age 3

Drafted to the US Army in Vietnam 9

Silvia and I Make a Life in Venezuela 70

About the Author 153

Colophon 155

Photographs and Mementos

winning a singles tournament. 1

racquet and ball in hand at two 3

Tennis Pro Walter Debany and the author. 4

the author and family in 1953. 6

the author and his family in the late 1950s 7

the author on graduation day from Tufts University. 8

the author in South Vietnam in 1970. 9

the author as company clerk in South Vietnam 25

Lieutenant George Drago and the author 26

a cookout in South Vietnam 28

US Army helicopters at Phu Bai, South Vietnam. 29

Top, first sergeant 31

A bridge leading to Hue, the old capital of Vietnam. 33

An old fortification near Hue 34

the walled city of Hue. 35

South Vietnamese houseboats lined up. 36

buddies in front of the (in)famous Steam Bath and Massage Parlor. 38

hooch girls from nearby villages. 41

two Vietnamese women who cleaned hooches 42

the author strumming his guitar 43

lining up in the hooch area 43

from the air during a chu hoi mission 45

accounting for every soldier 46

Sandy 51

Cool me enjoyed the sights and sounds of Hong Kong during R and R. ... 51

A restaurant in Victoria Harbour, Hong Kong. 52

A multitude of fishing boats in Victoria Harbour 52

Vietnamese residences near Eagle Beach 55

fishing guide 55

Eagle Beach on the South China Sea 56

How did she sneak into the base camp??? 57

volcanic mountains, Hawaii 58

headed to the grandstands for the Bob Hope Special 60

soldiers enjoyed the Bob Hope Special 61

an obscene sign in camp 63

captain, first sergeant, and two buddies. 65

the author atop a bunker outside the base at Phu Bai 66

the author's wife, Silvia, and the author at an old Spanish fort. 70

the author's father-in-law, Anibal Abreu .... 74, 76, and 77

Ernesto and Elbia Garcia 78

the author's wife at her job in Venezuelan educational television........79

a letter offering the author a job as tennis professional................80

a view of the Macuto Sheraton..81

the author and the hotel resident manager............................84

a view of the public beach and coastline.............................87

memories from El Litoral.......................................88 and 89

ranchos along the litoral..90

the blue Renault driven by the author and his wife...................92

Ron, Teresa, and their little boy, Hector, in December, 1982..........94

Ron, his co-best man Señor Bozo, and the author.....................96

Ron and Teresa with children, her mother, and the author.............97

getting ready for a tennis tournament................................99

a letter of resignation..100

Berlitz School headquarters in the Las Mercedes section of Caracas....101

the Berlitz branch school on Avenida Urdeneta in downtown Caracas....102

a Caracas food truck...103

the Venezuelan Foreign Minister and the author.......................105

Time magazine cover for author's Berlitz sessions with foreign minister..106

official authorization for admission to foreign minister's office....107

Plaza Bolivar in Caracas in front of Casa Amarilla...................108

Kanavayen Prado, the author's favorite restaurant....................109

the author's in-laws' apartment building in Caracas 111

the living room in the author's in-laws' Caracas apartment. 112

the author's mother-in-law and the author's wife. 113

Manny Trillo at bat. 115

the author's wife's cousin at work in a Venezuelan bullfight arena 116

the author's wife at a bullfight at Nuevo Circo 117

a ticket to the bullfight. 117

the crowd entering the bullfight arena at Maracay, top. 118

a bullfight begins. 118

a bull charges. 119

muleteers drag a dead bull. 119

the author's Venezuelan ID card. 123

memories from the Venezuelan island of Margarita . . . . 125 to 133

La Virgen del Valle Basilica on Margarita. .134 and 135

memories from Choroni . . . . 137 to 143

Silvia on the deck of chalet in the Selva Negra Hotel in La Colonia Tovar 145

a hotel and swimming pool at La Colonia Tovar 145

family mementos and photos . . . . 146 to 149

Mark Sydnor's protenis card 150

William Emrich. 153

In 1964, I won the singles title for players eighteen and under at the Shore & Country Club, Norwalk, Connecticut. I bested my opponent, the late Bruce Shadbolt, right.

a Prophetic Surprise Presentation

an introduction by William Emrich

  Little did I know that a surprise presentation to me some fifty years ago would turn out to be prophetic. The tennis program of the Norwalk, Connecticut, Shore & Country Club awarded me a wooden plaque with the inscription *Have Racquet, Will Travel,* words relevant in my life for the next twenty years.

  A tennis racquet traveled with me through my teenage years in Norwalk, then again through my undergraduate years at Tufts University in the Boston area, and then, remarkably, even into my service in the US Army, including fourteen months in war-torn South Vietnam. Upon my discharge from the military in 1971, *Have Racquet, Will Travel* journeyed with me back to Massachusetts and, years later, continued with me in my nearly two-year stay in Caracas, Venezuela, with my wife and her parents. I had no idea back in my late teens how the four inscribed words would weave into the fabric of my life for such a long time and in so many places.

I received the plaque at the annual tennis program awards dinner at Shore & Country Club. My family had a membership for many years and, in fact, my parents met there for the first time back in the late 1930s. When I received the plaque, I had just branched out from being a tennis player to teaching the sport there and at other area clubs. The club's tennis committee apparently wanted me to have the wooden plaque as acknowledgement of my entry into the world of teaching.

In the following pages, I will tell you about how time and circumstance fulfilled the plaque's prophecy as I traveled from Norwalk to Boston to South Vietnam to Caracas.

At two, in 1949, I had a racquet and ball in hand. By the time I was four, I had a presentable forehand, but this time, I whiffed.

at Home on the Courts from an Early Age

Not only did the Shore & Country Club employ me to teach tennis. Norwalk's Shorehaven Golf Club tennis pro gave me a job as his assistant, and I worked as fill-in pro at the Tokeneke Tennis Club in nearby Darien. I also taught tennis for the City of Norwalk Parks and Recreation Department in the summer during college breaks. I don't know what I would have done for employment during those many summers if I hadn't had the opportunity to work as a teaching tennis pro.

My family's membership in the Shore and Country Club provided me the opportunity to meet and later work with Walter Debany, who tremendously influenced and enriched my life. Walter was a lifelong bachelor and oldest son of a large Italian family, for whom he sacrificed a lot. He once confided that he spent so much time taking care of his younger brothers and sisters that he didn't have time to date. He was the head tennis professional for many years at the Shore & Country Club, where I spent almost all of my summers in my early years.

From the time I was five or six years old, I asked my mother or father to drive me to the club as early in the morning as possible because I really enjoyed spending time with the resident pro there; with Yudo Zanglein, the pro when I was younger, and then, with Walter during most of my teenage years. I especially enjoyed watching Walter prepare the clay tennis courts for use. Clay courts, preferred by most tennis enthusiasts, require much more maintenance than hard asphalt or cement courts. By the time the members arrived, all of the courts were in top-notch shape. Then he often headed over to his tennis shop to string racquets on a manual machine for club members who needed new strings in their racquets.

If a player wanted the string in the racquet at a particular level of tension, ol' Walter had a way of holding that string close to his ear, twinging it with his finger, and listening for a specific pitch that assured him he had satisfied the member's requirements. I loved watching him do that and, of course, would have tried to emulate him by using that same technique if I had strung my own racquets.

Tennis Pro Walter Debany took me under his wing at the club in 1956 when I was nine.

By my late teens, when Walter asked me to be his assistant tennis pro during the summer—an offer I readily accepted—a special treat was joining him for breakfast way back in the clubhouse's kitchen. Even though the cooks busied themselves preparing food for that day's menu, they always found time to cook up delicious breakfasts for the two of us. I never had eaten grits before, but I became an instant lover of them when chefs from the deep South cooked them as they were supposed to be cooked. As far as I could tell, all of the staff in that kitchen came from true southern states, and in my opinion, buttered grits with eggs, bacon, and toast constituted one of their best breakfast dishes, the source of my distinct pleasure every morning.

Once breakfast was over, Walter and I knew that club members would soon arrive, so we headed back to the tennis shop and courts. It wouldn't be long before Walter began his busy daily schedule of individual and group tennis lessons to members of all ages and ability. Often, I helped him during his lessons or watched the shop in his absence.

As Walter's assistant, I showed up before breakfast to prepare the courts for that day's play, something I had so often watched Walter do. My task included spraying the soft court surfaces with water. Later, I swept the courts with a wide broom to ensure a smooth surface before brushing off all the taped lines that defined specific sections of the courts.

Occasionally the clay courts became too dry from summer heat. Then I had to add lime manually in order to get the proper texture for an appropriate playing surface. That was a big and messy job, because the lime came in heavy-duty bags, each weighing probably a hundred pounds. Once I opened the bag, I had to load up a metal shovel with lime and sling it as smoothly and as far as I could to each area of the court. In hot summer sun, lime stuck to everything it touched, and it was a chore to keep it off my own body and clothes while I worked with it. I had to be very careful, because it would burn my skin if it touched any part of me. In spite of the challenge, lime always did the trick of providing just the right amount of moisture to the clay court's surface.

Once the courts were watered, swept, and cleaned, I always looked forward to meeting Walter in the clubhouse kitchen to enjoy that delicious breakfast I already described. I was, without a doubt, an extremely fortunate young man to be able to have such an experience during my summers back then. Walter and I stayed in touch in the off-season by occasionally sending each other letters. However, In March, 1968, as I studied in my college dormitory in Massachusetts, I got a call from the head of the club's tennis committee. Walter had passed away at the untimely age of forty-nine. He had died in his New York home of a heart attack. To be sure, it was a tremendous personal loss for me, and I miss him dearly to this day.

At three, above, I'm with my mother, Marjorie, and my sister, Susan, at the Shore & Country Club. My family in the middle 1950s, from left, included my father, Emerson; my mother, Marjorie; my sisters Jean, Donna, and Susan; and me.

My dad and I paused from swimming at the club in 1953, top left; we were on the courts in the late 1950s at the club, top right; we're dressed up to go somewhere when I was ten, bottom left; my sister Susan and I waited with our racquets at the club when I was thirteen, bottom right.

In spring, 1969, top, I posed for my senior picture on the roof at Wessell Library, Tufts University, during our graduation weekend when I received my bachelor's degree in political science.

With a backdrop of Vietnamese landscape, I'm hot and sweaty in Southeast Asian heat.

Drafted to the US Army in Vietnam

My sheltered and privileged life changed considerably when in 1969, just months after I graduated with a political science undergraduate degree from Tufts University, my number came up in the draft lottery. I was due to be inducted into the US Army. In those years, the United States had hundreds of thousands of troops in South Vietnam fighting the Viet Cong and North Vietnamese. Anti-war demonstrators in the States made their voices heard in an increasingly powerful and persuasive way.

Although I knew of ways intentionally to fail the Army's physical test or even to avoid military service altogether by moving to Canada as some members of my generation had done, I did not seriously consider those options. It wasn't long before I passed the physical in September, three months after graduation, and faced military service for a minimum of twenty-four months. I was thrown into the military world that I knew little about and wasn't emotionally prepared for. How *Have Racquet, Will Travel* would fit into the next two years of my life is a surprising story that I am about to share with you, if you are willing to hear me out.

Day One at Basic Training

Once I was shuffled into a long line entering the reception Station at Fort Dix, New Jersey, I pretty much stayed in long lines for the rest of the day. The army measured us draftees for our uniforms and boots, examined us to see if we were medically qualified to be in the Army, gave each of us a haircut (if you could call it that—it was more like a head-shave, leaving very little hair on the top of our head), and required us to take any number of written and oral tests and quizzes.

One quiz involving my eyesight quickly revealed I am color-blind. That discovery completely surprised me. The examiner had asked me to tell him what numbers I saw on the pages of a booklet, and when I told him I couldn't see any numbers on the page, that proved my color blindness to him because I could not see the color red when on a dark background. In all of my twenty-two years to that point on Planet Earth, I had not noticed that condition nor, thankfully, had it caused me any problems with driving or other activity. And apparently it wouldn't cause me any difficulties within the military, either, because I never heard any more about it during the rest of my time in the Army.

My head spun a bit by the end of that first day of basic training. It didn't help that, when I tried on my infantry boots for the first time, they were at least one size too small. Every time that I walked in them, my big toes cramped up and hurt like hell. But I didn't want to complain, because the last thing I wanted was to be noticed by the guys in charge or, even worse, be labeled a complainer. I put up with that painful discomfort for the entirety of basic training, but if I had to do it again (God forbid), I would definitely have asked my sergeant if I could get a pair of boots that actually fit.

First Week of Basic Training

After being assigned to a training company, I got a bunk bed in one of many barracks on base and looked around to see who I would be spending the next eight weeks of my life with. Basically, it appeared to be a group of young men of many different nationalities and races. I didn't care about that. What I did care about was how I would get along with those guys and if I could find a few who would turn out to be my buddies as we went through the stressful and challenging situation we found ourselves in.

In the barracks, our bunk area housed four men to a section, and after a couple of days, I felt relieved that the three other draftees in my group seemed like good guys. One was married, and his wife would soon give birth to twins. One had arrived in the United States from Italy six months before and now, barely able to speak or understand the English language, found himself in the US Army, and believe me, he wasn't happy about it. One, came from New Jersey, I think, and worried about his ability to handle the physical challenges of training. Fortunately for him, the physical part of basic training didn't start until the second week, so at least he had a few days to prepare himself for what lay ahead.

That first week, we learned basic military functions, such as how to stand and march in formation, how to respond properly to the training sergeant's orders, and what we had to do in terms of cleanliness and orderliness in our barracks. I know that I was not pleased to hear from our drill sergeant that each one of us in that company would be called to lead the company for a day. Before I even started basic, friends who had spent time in the military advised me that the single best way to act in that first eight weeks at Fort Dix was not to be noticed. Never sit or stand at the start or end of any formation, and never volunteer for anything. That sounded like good advice to me, but I found myself facing the prospect of having to lead the entire company sometime during our two months of training.

Especially when standing in formation at the start of each day, I kept my head low, tried to be in the middle of any line (and believe me, we were always in line for something), and definitely never volunteered to help out in any way. That strategy seemed to work out well for me, but one day I had to do one of the classic basic training activities: peeling potatoes at the mess hall. I remember the camp cook telling me to go to the back of his cooking tent with a huge bucket of potatoes and start peeling. I peeled and peeled and then peeled some more. I didn't mind the job too much, but I didn't like the feeling of being separated from the rest of my company because I didn't want to miss whatever the other draftees learned that day. As it turned out, I don't think that I missed anything critical, because I meshed with my fellow trainees the next day without any problem.

Second Week of Basic Training

Because we draftees got only about four or five hours of sleep a night and our bodies hadn't yet adjusted to it, we all functioned on adrenalin alone. Relentless training continued as we learned basic marksmanship skills with a rifle, proper use of a bayonet, and army drill procedures. Use my bayonet in a close-combat situation? I am not at all sure that the minimal training I received for using that weapon would sufficiently prepare me to be victorious in a life or death struggle. But I suppose we trainees had to, at the very least, be introduced to bayonet use as part of our overall instruction on effective use of our standard infantry weapons.

I found one bit of unplanned instruction very unpleasant. Before our drill sergeant called us to line up in formation in the early morning hours of each day, we had to leave our bed area and personal items in top military shape and properly secured. On the morning in question, I don't know why, but I apparently left my metal locker unlocked before hurrying outside. When my name got called during formation, the charge officer ordered me to run several times in a big circle around my entire company while loudly singing some stupid song about getting caught being sloppy with my personal gear. It was a humiliating exercise in front of my fellow trainees, and, as was intended, made me vow to never again leave my assigned locker unsecured.

Third Week of Basic Training

We increased our marksmanship skills with both the M-14 and M-16 rifles with live ammunition instead of simulated rounds. We also received instruction in how to locate proper targets on the battlefield and then hit them with effective firepower. Initially, I had problems with this phase of the training because the muscles in my left eye are much stronger than those in my right eye. When I attempted to sight a target with my right eye, my normal eye for shooting, the image appeared very distorted. I couldn't sight my rifle correctly. Using a patch over my left eye resolved the problem, but that wouldn't work in a real-life combat situation, so I eventually taught my left eye to close for sufficient time to sight my rifle with my right eye. Once that situation resolved, I turned out to be an accurate and effective shooter of both types of rifles.

While I prepared to fire my rifle on the range one day, one of the sergeants came over and told me that he knew I had been a teaching tennis professional. He seemed intrigued by the discovery. I wondered how he had learned about my tennis past, and then I began to wonder how I might be able to turn that experience into doing something similar in the Army. However, neither the sergeant nor I brought that subject up again during the basic eight weeks of training. Still, *Have Racquet, Will Travel* had somehow extended itself into my time in the military, if only in a conversational way. Later I will share with you how it showed up again in a more realistic, active way that I would never have envisioned after three weeks of basic training.

Fourth Week of Basic Training

During this week, an extension of the previous week's training, we were all tested and our scores recorded as to how well we shot the M-14 and M-16 rifles. We got hands-on advice about how we could improve our accuracy and our knowledge of the makeup of the weapons themselves. We had instruction on how to take apart our rifles, clean them, and put them back together, and we learned how to take care of them properly in the field. I think that at that point in the training, all of us in the company began to think of ourselves as infantry soldiers, a big change in self-image from just a month earlier.

Fifth Week of Basic Training

We spent days learning not only basic first aid procedures but also the use of hand grenades, the effects of chemical warfare on the mind and body, and some essential infantry tactics in the field of battle. Throwing my first live hand grenade proved an interesting experience, to say the least. The instructors told us to run up to a sandbagged bunker, grab one of the grenades placed there, pull the ring from it, count a few numbers, and then toss the darned thing towards the target in an open field.

Sounds easy, right? Well, holding on to a grenade even for one second after you have pulled its all-important ring does not constitute my idea of a walk in the park. Holding on to it for more than one second focuses attention very sharply. Thank goodness I had to throw only one live grenade, because my nerves would have been fried by the time I tossed just two or three.

One fellow draftee waiting his turn at this necessary but stressful exercise made fun of the way I ran to the bunker with the grenades. Hey! At that point, I didn't care about how I ran. I just wanted to be sure to remember to toss that damned thing before it exploded into pieces of shrapnel.

As for training we received in countering the effects of chemical warfare, I didn't enjoy that, either. One by one, every draftee in my company had to enter a warehouse-type building wearing a gas mask. Then, as each of us stood in the building, we had to take off the gas masks and consequently expose ourselves to a cloud of tear gas. After taking in the effects of noxious gas for a few seconds, we could exit the building. Funny that not a single draftee walked out of the building. All of us ran like hell for the nearest door. Tear gas stings your eyes something awful, and a person's body has a major negative reaction to the gas's chemical makeup.

The live grenade exercise and painful personal exposure to a toxic gas as an introduction to chemical warfare unquestionably comprised memorable times for all of us in basic training. When the weekend arrived, though, our first allowable time off the base helped to considerably counter difficult experiences. We could leave Fort Dix on Saturday morning and not return until Sunday evening. A buddy from my bunk area and I arranged for two female friends from Massachusetts to drive down to our base in New Jersey and stay with us for those precious thirty-six hours of freedom.

We met the young women at the base and quickly found two rooms at a hotel in the area. However, my lack of sleep and tough physical conditions of training finally caught up with me, and I arrived at the hotel worn out and with a burning fever. Miraculously, within a couple of hours off base with my friends, my fever broke. I felt like a new man. Apparently, a part of me would not let that weekend of freedom and friends go to waste.

Sixth Week of Basic Training

Training continued improving on our infantryman skills with instruction on how to move effectively and as safely as possible on a battlefield. We learned how to assault an enemy position as a team along with the importance of communicating directly and understandably with fellow soldiers when approaching the enemy under combat conditions.

We each grew more comfortable with carrying and using our assigned weapons, too. Finally, we received instruction on how to infiltrate an area effectively without being detected by the enemy. This latest skill probably improved our ability to sneak over to the commissary after-hours to refill our supplies of cigarettes, snacks, and drinks when we were supposed to be in our barracks. I always worried we would get caught, but maybe infiltration training gave us draftees just the edge we needed not to be spotted by one of the sergeants.

Seventh Week of Basic Training

With only two weeks of basic training to go, physical challenges increased with different individual exercises on the bayonet assault course as well as something called the confidence course. Translated, that means a heck of a lot of running around, through, under, and over obstacles placed in front of you within a set period of time. For any overweight guys in my company or any not physically nimble, this part of training posed considerable difficulty. Fortunately, slim and used to running and jogging, I did not find this part of the program too bothersome.

I remember one poor soul, one of the four of my original group in the barracks, who must have felt the week as personal torture for him, especially when doing pull-ups on a bar. Whether because of something physical or a mental block or even a combination of the two, the man struggled mightily at those bars. Frankly, I don't know if he ever managed to complete those pull-ups, but he gave it his all.

We all have our individual hang-ups, so I could empathize with the guy. Mine showed up during my military service in the form of stuttering or blocking on certain words to the point where no sound would come out. And believe it or not, it would occur whenever I had to call out my name. You would think that your own name would be a comfortable and easy thing to say, but man, not in my case. I had a certain hang-up on words starting with the letter e. With my formal first name, Emerson, every time we were in military formation, the block haunted me. Our sergeant told us to call out our first name after he called our last name in order to be marked present. It always caused a traumatic moment for me. Most times I would somehow smudge my way through it by putting an s in front of my name as I called out.

I remember a time much later in the service when the top brass on our overseas base did unannounced checks of company personnel. They apparently had a problem with soldiers not being where they should be on the base. I responded to their late-night call for everybody in our company to stand in formation outside of our hooches. They called my last name, and I literally could not make a sound come out of my mouth. They called my last name a second time, and again I tried but failed not only to call out my first name but even to make any sound at all. God only knows what the rest of my company thought, because they all stood there in formation with me.

It embarrassed me beyond belief, but no one ever mentioned the incident or asked what had happened. I wonder to this day what my fellow soldiers thought went on with me as I stood in total silence. So, yeah, I think I knew how badly the traumatized draftee felt by having to do a required number of pull-ups as part of his training. Reliving his trauma in my own painful way, I had no trouble relating to what he went through.

Eighth Week of Basic Training

The final week! We underwent proficiency testing in the many skills taught since Day One at Fort Dix. By the time the week came to a close, we prepared for graduation ceremonies. Since I had been inducted into the Army, I had no idea what I would be doing or where I would be doing it for the next two or three months, never mind the next almost two years. I was so happy and relieved to be done with basic training that it didn't concern me much when I received orders to report in a few short days for advanced infantry training. I would have a specialty in indirect fire, more commonly known as mortars, at Fort Lewis near Tacoma, Washington, on the Pacific coast, close to majestic Mount Rainier. I didn't know it then, but I would get to know Mount Rainier up close and personal in a few weeks' time under some pretty terrible physical conditions. Right then, though, I thought about little else except enjoying a few days of freedom before reporting for my flight to the northwest part of our country and the start of my advanced infantry training.

Advanced Infantry Training

If I thought Basic Training at Fort Dix qualified as arduous and challenging, then I had to double or triple that assessment when it came to my time in AIT. For one thing, terrible weather lasted throughout the more than two months I was out there. Almost daily, surface winds and moisture-laden clouds hit the chain of mountains that parallel the Pacific coastline near Fort Lewis, resulting in miserable outdoor conditions.

Most of the time we trained outside and experienced cold temperatures mixed with lots of rain. I remember a horrible time when we bivouacked on the side of the mountain. During the day, we practiced setting up our mortars and preparing them for firing. When darkness approached, we had to set up our tents wherever we could find a suitable spot on the severe incline. Not surprisingly, it started to rain just as we pitched the tents. Despite digging trenches around our two-man tents to direct rainwater away, my tent mate and I soon discovered the tent situated at such an extreme angle that torrents of water rushed down the mountainside into our tent. We could not get away from the cold wind and constant rush of muddy water, so ever so gently, I slipped my fully clothed, drenched body into my equally soaked sleeping bag and tried to sleep. I doubt I got any sleep under those conditions, but all I could think of was to make it through that disaster until sunrise. It had to be one of the most uncomfortable nights of my life. I would never again look at snow-capped Mount Rainier the same way.

Another horrible episode I experienced at Fort Lewis, I will tell you about so that, after all of these years, I can finally vent. One of our AIT training exercises involved all of us learning to escape from enemy captivity. The designated "enemy" would march each of us in the company from Point A to Point B, and presumably we would figure out a way to escape during the march.

To prepare, we viewed a map that showed where we would start as well as the rendezvous point that hopefully we would all reach after successfully escaping from the bad guys. A company buddy hatched a plan for both of us to break rank and run into some woods just as the captive company made a big turn in the road leading to the enemy camp. I agreed to try it with him, and sure enough, we both ducked into the woods at the appointed time.

And then my troubles started.

In the darkness, I couldn't locate my buddy, and I couldn't call out to him for fear of getting recaptured. After trying to reconnect with him and not having any luck, I realized I would have to try to get to the rendezvous point on my own. I headed through the woods in the direction I thought would get me there, but my usual good sense of direction failed me that night. I ended up in what appeared to be a big, fenced-off cow field and had no idea where to go next. By then, it was the middle of the night, and the only light I had came from the moon and stars.

I did not have a pleasant feeling out there in the dark alone and with no knowledge of where I was. After wandering around for a few more minutes trying to get my bearings, I decided I would just sit down and wait for some help. I heard a vehicle approaching in the distance and thought my company would locate me and bring me back to safety. That was a completely wrong assumption, as I found out soon enough.

When I called to the people in the vehicle, they drove over to where I stood. The same "enemy" I had earlier escaped from recaptured me. They drove me to a small camp nearby designated strictly for prisoners and interrogated me for the next couple of hours. They forced me to run in circles carrying a large, heavy log on my shoulders and generally gave me an extremely unpleasant time. Later, when they let me rejoin my fellow trainees, I realized the successful escapees enjoyed a good ol' time back at the camp while I endured a night of disorientation and punishment. It took me a while to process that miserable experience, especially since I think I was the only escapee recaptured that night.

By the time AIT ended and we celebrated another graduation, we had undergone thorough training in the use of the M-16 and our specialty, mortars. Those weapons of indirect fire were heavy and cumbersome to carry, and I remember one rather small fellow draftee assigned to carry the big metal ring that provides a stable platform for firing. We had headed off on a scheduled long march through the countryside. The poor guy had put the heavy ring over his head and resting on both shoulders as we started off. He must have tripped as we hiked down a steep hill. Suddenly, he and that heavy metal ring came crashing down the hill, and both landed in a big heap at the bottom of our hiking path. Once the guy lost his balance, he was a goner with that metal contraption around his neck. The rest of us had to keep marching along, so I don't know if he got seriously hurt or not, but the image I had of him and his heavy ring rolling down the hill has stayed with me all of these years.

Another time in AIT, I made the unpardonable infantry mistake of not keeping my assigned M-16 rifle with me at all times. At the conclusion of another long march, we had to set up our tents in a wooded area not far from the base of Mount Rainier. As I started to put the tent together, I placed my rifle on the side of a tree just a couple of feet away. A sergeant walked by my area, and he quickly confiscated my weapon. In no uncertain terms, I learned I had committed a grievous error—an infantryman having his weapon taken away—and for several days I did not have permission to carry my rifle with me.

That may not sound like much of a punishment, but if you are in advanced infantry training and denied permission to carry a weapon during instruction periods and exercises, it definitely feels like a big deal. Needless to say, no one ever again separated me from my M-16.

The AIT we received included an introduction to the standard 50-caliber machine gun, a large and deadly weapon of twentieth-century warfare. We also learned about the M-79 grenade launcher and M-60 machine gun as well as about a hand-held, shoulder-launched, anti-tank weapon, that allowed an individual soldier in battle to have at least a fighting chance against an enemy tank. I fired one of those surprisingly portable weapons at an old wreck of a tank placed a good distance away from where we trainees stood. I was amazed not only by its accuracy but also by the loud and substantial blast of air that erupted from the back of the weapon when it fired.

You definitely would not want to stand close behind any soldier firing one of those projectiles. You would not want to be inside a tank in an exposed area and within range of that anti-tank round, either. Fearsome beasts, the 50-caliber machine gun and the shoulder-launched, anti-tank weapon quickly gain respect. Most of the specialized weapon's training that we received those many weeks in the fields and forests of Fort Lewis, Washington, however, centered on the sharpening of our skills in the setting up and firing of the mortar.

Mortars require two persons to fire a round accurately and effectively. It turned out that the young man assigned as the other half of my training team ended up a good friend for the next several weeks of training. You could tell that Michael was a smart guy right from the start. He became the more skilled member of our two-man team when it came to firing a mortar round accurately to a specific area and target. I was glad that he was on my team when it came to the proficiency tests we were required to pass before graduation. And later, when we deployed overseas, Michael and I stayed in touch and eventually spent an unforgettable week together in Hong Kong as part of our Rest and Recreation privileges, called R&R in the Army. More on that later.

Despite intense and challenging infantry training in the harsh winter conditions of the Pacific Northwest, I somehow did manage to fulfill the requirements of AIT. All of a sudden one morning in early 1970, I found myself along with the rest of my company lined up in military formation before a base commander on the graduation field. To our left stood another company of graduating trainees and a similar group to our right. We were all there in formation not only to celebrate our graduation but also to receive our orders about where we would spend the next and most important part of our military service no longer as infantry trainees but as US soldiers.

In 1970, the war in South Vietnam still raged with high casualties on both sides. The United States needed to replace troops lost to injury or death as well as the ones who had put in required service time and had to be sent home. Therefore, there was a very good chance that all three companies lined up before the base commander would be sent to Vietnam for the next twelve months. I was not at all surprised when the commander told us over the loudspeaker that our company would be ordered to report in a few days to be flown to Da Nang Air Base in South Vietnam to begin our overseas tour of duty.

Even though I expected the order, it was still a very sobering piece of news. I did not know what to think about being an infantry soldier in that far-off country for the next year. But then I was completely flabbergasted when the orders for the other two companies in formation were announced. The one to my left pulled Germany for their tour of duty, and the one to my right would go to South Korea. Are you #!*&+%! kidding me? My company would go to the brutal war in South Vietnam while two thirds of my fellow draftees would spend their service time in Germany and in South Korea?

I just could not believe their luck and my misfortune. How did I happen to end up in the one company going to an active war zone? I would find out later that my best buddy, Sonny from basic training at Fort Dix, got assigned to show motion pictures to the troops on his base in Germany. My other friend, Bob from the eight weeks at Fort Dix, would be a radio operator in Seoul. I was livid. I definitely felt sorry for myself, but there was nothing I could do about the forbidding situation I found myself in.

Within about ten days of receiving orders, I reported for duty at a military base in California and got on a plane that took me halfway across the globe to a foreign country and culture unlike any I had ever experienced.

Oppressive and overwhelming heat hit me as I stepped down the stairs of the plane onto the tarmac of huge Da Nang military base and took my first breath in South Vietnam. The air felt heavy and stifling hot. There was no way a person could not notice and react to it. That heat remained my constant companion wherever I went in Vietnam during my many months in country. Even during the amazing monsoon season when rain poured from the sky hour after hour and day after day, that oppressive hot air stayed with me.

Not more than a couple of hours after I stepped off that airplane in Da Nang, I embarrassed myself by revealing my naïveté about the war I had been sent by my country to fight. Our superiors in South Vietnam shuffled many other newcomers and me into a bus to transport us through the city to some other military camp in the area. As the driver tried to navigate the busy streets filled with people on rickshaws, bicycles, small cars, motorbikes, and motorcycles, I noticed all of the windows of our bus covered by metal screens. I asked the soldier seated next to me, who appeared to be a veteran of the war and not a newcomer like me, the reason for the screens.

He turned and looked at me as if I had just come from another planet—and not a particularly intelligent planet at that. He said, "Those screens are to deflect any hand grenades tossed at the window by the enemy as they pass by on motorcycles."

I felt like a complete fool for asking the question. Right there it hit me that I had landed in a real war with real people trying to kill me in any way they could. Up to that point of my barely six months of military service, while I would not have chosen the experience, I had treated the time as an obligation to my country more than anything else. Consequently, even though I arrived in Vietnam as an infantry soldier, I viewed my new surroundings more like a curious visitor to a new and very different foreign land than as a setting that threatened my very survival. The blunt answer I received to my innocent question from that veteran soldier changed all that.

Undoubtedly it established a crucial change to my way of thinking as well as my behavior in the days and months ahead. I needed to make the change immediately and for as long as I stayed in war-torn South Vietnam. Changing became even more imperative because of the impossibility of distinguishing by appearance alone friend from enemy in many places in that country. The men, women, or even children who looked innocent enough a few feet away from you could in fact carry a weapon or explosive device under their clothing or in a decorative bag. During your interactions with those same people in the daytime, they indeed appeared innocent enough. But when darkness set in, that nice young Vietnamese man selling fruits and nuts by the side of the road could very well change his clothing into all-black Viet Cong garb and try to slide under your base camp's barbed wire to attack you. To be unaware of the danger posed simply because you were an American soldier anywhere in that country could get you killed or maimed very quickly. For the most part I lived out my days there with that new and stark realization clearly on my mind, but a little later I will tell you about two times when I foolishly forgot that I had to keep that realization foremost in my thoughts. One of those times it almost cost me big-time.

In-Country Training

Once officially in South Vietnam, I entered a week of in-country training that the Army required for arrivals in the war zone before sending newcomers out into the so-called boonies where most combat action took place. One week of so called in-country training filled the bill for my fellow infantrymen and me, all of us just arrived in that war zone.

We learned specifics on techniques of jungle warfare, such as how to avoid a variety of booby traps as you patrolled the countryside, how not to give away your position at night by foolishly lighting a cigarette, and how to remain constantly on alert for the enemy's use of tunnels. Also, our superiors emphasized the importance of taking care of small cuts and bruises due to the great danger of infection in that hot, humid climate. We learned about the necessity of taking a malaria pill every day and the advisability of maintaining good overall personal hygiene. Of course, maintaining good hygiene while in a jungle setting with no clean running water and plenty of bugs, insects, and assorted bacteria served often more as a goal than a reality, but our superiors strongly advised us to try.

Finally, as part of our in-country training, we had to enter a forbidding-looking tunnel dug in the ground expressly to give each of us a taste of dealing with the large number of tunnels built and used with great effectiveness by the enemy throughout the countryside. Once inside the narrow tunnel in total darkness, we had to follow our fellow soldiers by crawling on our hands and knees until we reached the opening on the other end.

I found the experience excruciating because of my tendency toward claustrophobia in situations much less severe. I had to fight to control a feeling of increasing panic while at the same time trying to trust that the soldier in front of me knew where he was going. Getting through that darkened tunnel amounted to a major achievement for me. I still almost get the chills when I think about it.

Perhaps on the final day of our in-country training, we went through a course set up to simulate dangers that we should expect from enemy forces in the field. The enemy might string wires across your expected path that set off explosive devices when tripped by a passing soldier. Or the enemy might dig a large hole, outfit the bottom with punji sticks, an array of finely sharpened bamboo sticks sometimes topped with manure, and camouflage the hole. Punji sticks would tear into the flesh of any soldier that fell in.

Then we learned about the pop-up mine, so named because when stepped on by an unsuspecting soldier, it would literally jump up into the air before exploding into deadly bits of shrapnel, thus causing maximum damage to the victim's body. The enemy had even devised the real-life, pop-up enemy soldier who would see your unit approaching and wait unseen in a camouflaged hole in the ground or in a hole that led to a much larger tunnel deep in the ground. Then that individual would wait until he thought he had maximum advantage to show himself and fire off a few deadly rounds at point-blank range.

Naturally, all of the week's training constituted a sobering introduction to what lay ahead for those of us headed to the combat situation in that tragic and brutal war zone.

Okay. It was time to take the next step. I had received all the training and orientation that a new infantryman in South Vietnam would get, so the next step meant finding out my assignment and its location for the major part of my tour of duty.

Was it going to be in the southern part of the country where acres upon acres of rice paddies covered the landscape throughout the region?

Was it going to be in the northern section of the country, a land of numerous, well-forested mountains? The mountains provided cover for countless North Vietnamese forces secretively and effectively using the Ho Chi Minh Trail to bring soldiers, food, and weapons into the heart of South Vietnam.

Over approximately two weeks, I received orders to report to a series of increasingly smaller and smaller combat units, each time going farther and farther to the north, until one day I found myself standing in a small formation of maybe not more than thirty soldiers. I realized that each one of us standing there would receive our final orders informing us what we would be doing and where. I assumed that I would be assigned to mortar duty in combat. This was it. I faced a minimum of six months in the extremely dangerous boonies—and maybe more.

Then, out of the blue, the officer barked out to us, "Can anyone here type? We need two men who can type." I couldn't believe my ears. I could type. I had actually taken a typing class in high school and done well at it. It turned out one of the most helpful classes I took in public school. I raised my hand, and another guy in the formation did, too. The officer called the two of us over and told us we would be sent to a unit of the 101st Airborne Division, Airmobile, stationed at Landing Zone Sallie near the Demilitarized Zone, or DMZ, a narrow strip of land officially separating North Vietnam and South Vietnam. A headquarters unit of the US Army Division known as the Screaming Eagles had put in a request for two soldiers who could type.

Believe me, it made me very happy to oblige them. Filled with uncertainty about my feelings about being thrust by my own federal government into the almost certain combat environment of "kill or be killed," of receiving a direct order to "kill the enemy," an enemy that I only recognized as my enemy because my government said so, I had no problem at all choosing a non-combatant role in the US Army if given the chance. Up to that point since my induction, I didn't feel I had a choice in the matter. Here, though, I had a chance to volunteer as a typist and effectively choose whether I would be in the field in a direct combat role or at a base camp somewhere in a supportive position. I quickly volunteered. If I had preferred direct combat, I simply would not have let that officer know I could type. I am certain my original orders would have assigned me to an Army combat unit.

Sure, a part of me would have liked for me to be seen as a warrior with all the strength and manly heroism that personifies, but I also realized that the fantasy of being that kind of a figure often turns out very different than imagined. If I could honorably and faithfully serve my country without having to deal with a direct combat order to kill the enemy, then I would choose that option. And I did. The federal government asks a helluva lot of a person when it orders him or her to kill another human being it identifies as the adversary. In my mind, the identified adversary had better be, without question, a true enemy of the state and a serious danger to the country. Otherwise, for a fraudulent reason, the government commits an unforgiveable injustice upon that citizen's humanity by ordering him or her to kill a fellow human being, an act grave, far-reaching, and irreversible.

If at that moment when I received my final in-country deployment orders I had been assigned to combat instead of a US Army supportive role, I believe I would probably have felt it my duty, after being put in a combat situation, to follow orders to engage and kill the enemy. I will in all likelihood never know for sure what I would have done.

However, an earlier experience I had when I first entered the country revealed what I probably would have done in the future. I had been assigned to guard duty at a camp where I was temporarily stationed. After a few hours of sitting in the darkness around a bunker, I received an order to fire a grenade from an M-79 launcher to a spot outside the perimeter where possible enemy movement had been detected. I hesitated to carry out the order because of the conflict I have just described raging within me. However, I finally did fire that grenade to the designated area, which showed no results. So apparently, the possible enemy movement had been a false alarm.

In reality, I dodged a bullet in more ways than one when that officer stood before my formation and asked if any of us could type.

Within a short time, the other volunteer typist and I found ourselves reporting for duty at LZ Sallie. I have very few recollections of that small helicopter base in the far northern reaches of South Vietnam, because just about the time I was starting to settle in there, our entire unit was ordered to deploy to a much larger base camp farther south. But I do remember that the first night I was there, a fellow soldier (who I soon learned was the company's designated librarian) took me under his wing and brought me with him to watch a movie being shown to the troops in an open area of the camp.

Halfway through the movie, the film broke in the projector, something I was told occurred often during that particular LZ's attempt at entertaining the troops. After a while, I almost got used to the many times the movie film broke during a showing. The soldier manning the projector always did his best to splice the pieces of film together hastily so the movie-going troops could see the movie through to completion.

The next day, the company's first sergeant, Charles DeLucia, or Top to those in the unit, showed me the office where I would type and essentially act as assistant to the company clerk. Although the number of soldiers in a company varied, a typical number in Vietnam was about 140. Top told me I would be expected to work in that office seven days a week, mostly typing official letters and documents on behalf of the headquarters company. I would also answer the phone during the day and help keep a record of the whereabouts of every soldier in our unit.

Out of respect to soldiers fighting in the field, I would have no days off. However, the strict dress code for soldiers back in the States relaxed now that we were in an overseas' war zone, and we could do whatever we wanted in the evening or at night as long as we stayed within the camp's security perimeter. Big sandbag bunkers stood everywhere, and on the ground and frequently in the skies were helicopters of all descriptions. Multiple rolls of concertina wire and deadly Claymore mines surrounded the perimeter of the camp, illuminated at night by flares shot high into the sky every few seconds by

I did my thing as company clerk for Headquarters Company.

the indirect fire guys. The flares lit the sky up nicely but only for a few seconds before slowly falling back to earth attached to a small parachute.

I didn't notice those parachuting flares much at night back in my barracks, or hooch, as it was called. But when I pulled regular guard duty around the camp perimeter at night, it made me happy to have those tiny sparkling lights slowly falling to the ground several yards out in front. Otherwise, I couldn't see a thing through the pitch black beyond the barbed wire and mines. Knowing that the enemy could breach the wires and mines we set out to protect us, I felt very thankful that those parachuting flares gave me a good chance of spotting sappers who might approach the perimeter. Only seconds passed between the light from one flare dying as it fell to the ground and another flare sent high to light up the sky. In the few seconds with no illumination, my imagination ran wild as to who might be out there in that darkness with the deadliest of intentions.

I mentioned earlier that soon after my arrival our headquarters company (HHC, 2nd Brigade, 101st Airborne Division, Airmobile) had orders to vacate LZ Sallie and relocate to a bigger base camp farther south in Phu Bai. The camp was near the

Lieutenant George Drago and I took a minute in front of the sign for our HHC unit in Vietnam in 1970.

ancient capital city of Hue, site of fierce fighting during the famous Tet Offensive a couple of years before we arrived.

In order for us to move from one camp to another, we had to pack practically everything in our headquarters' office and drive it by truck and Jeep to the new site in Phu Bai. And here's where I received a really unpleasant public dressing down from my boss, Top. I made the mistake of loading my typewriter in the bed of our truck. Then I sat down in the passenger seat for the long, bumpy ride south.

When Top saw where I had placed my typewriter, he blew a fuse. He yelled and screamed that the typewriter must ride with me in my lap, and nothing had better happen along our trip to damage it in any way. Even though Top was probably right about the need to keep the typewriter in good condition during the long ride along dusty and lousy roads, I couldn't believe what a tantrum he threw. Unfortunately, I would see a lot of similar behavior over the coming months from him. Even when his venom singled out others, it was never pleasant.

Well, my typewriter and I thankfully made it in good condition to our new home in Phu Bai, a much more complete and established base camp for the 101st Airborne Division. We quickly settled in to our new quarters. Right across from our hooches, a big building housed showers not so luxurious nor welcoming as to have hot water. At least they gave us a way to keep ourselves reasonably clean, and a cold shower certainly did wake you up in the morning almost as well as a cup of coffee. Not far from the showers, we ate three meals a day cafeteria style in the mess hall, and I have to say that we ate very well. We had a surprisingly good variety and quality of food. Also, if you were fortunate enough to know a buddy who knew a buddy who in turn knew a guy who worked in the kitchen, you'd be amazed at how often you could barbeque up a steak dinner right next to your hooch.

Most of the hooches, basically tin-roofed sleeping areas on three-foot stilts, housed from six to eight soldiers. Each man guarded his bed and few feet of individual space very closely. Some of the guys covered their small area with a sheet or blanket for more privacy while others didn't seem to put privacy high on their priorities. Everybody had different hours when they preferred to hit the sack, however, and given the tight quarters and tendency of some men to socialize and party into the wee hours of the night, getting enough sleep posed a challenge for me some nights.

But, frankly, the guys in my hooch lived remarkably well together and got along fine. I mean, here was a bunch of guys from different backgrounds and life styles thrown together in a foreign land for months at a time, and I can't remember a single

We enjoyed a nice cookout, maybe to celebrate a fellow soldier going home the next day.

knockdown/drag-out physical fight. Remarkable really, and very fortunate, because not far from us a group of hooches housed infantry soldiers in from the field for a few days at a time. Decidedly more volatile, conditions there became, yes, even dangerous, compared to our headquarters' housing area.

The big base in Phu Bai held an untold number of combat helicopters and other formidable weapons of war. The helicopters lined up in individual bunkers to protect them as much as possible from incoming mortar rounds. I recall one day when I heard shouting and looked up into the sky just in time to see a copter in obvious trouble trying to reach the safety of our camp perimeter. All of a sudden, it turned completely over in the air, dropped, and then disappeared from my sight. I heard later that enemy ground fire wounded the pilot outside of the base, and that the wounded pilot was trying desperately to fly the copter back to camp. From what I witnessed, however, he and his crew had little chance of survival after the chopper turned upside down in the air. No one in my headquarters company was involved in the attempted rescue of the crew because the base camp was so large. A half mile or more separated us from the tragedy. The image of that helicopter and its crew trying mightily but unsuccessfully to land safely within our base has stayed with me all these many years. Of course, I pray that the crewmen of that chopper beat the odds and survived.

During my assignment to the Phu Bai base camp, reports surfaced of fragging of officers or sergeants in their bed, causing widespread concern. Fragging means that a soldier of lesser rank bore some grievance against his superior in command while they were in the field together and then used a deadly fragmentation grenade as his weapon of revenge.

So-called fragging could be carried out for any number of reasons. It could be racially motivated: many lower ranking grunts in the boonies were African Americans, while their ranking superiors often were Caucasian. It could be because the perpetrator didn't like an order he had received, especially if that order put him in imminent danger. It could be because a soldier felt he was being unfairly picked on by his officer. Honestly, it could be due to any kind of grievance, real or imagined, that a soldier suffered while risking his life out in the field. When he and his company came back to the base camp, as nighttime arrived and the members of his unit went to their respective beds, it wouldn't take much effort for a crazed individual seeking revenge to roll a live fragmentation grenade under the bed of the officer who supposedly caused his suffering. Reportedly that type of incident had occurred way too frequently. Naturally, fragging had everyone in camp on edge.

US Army helicopters lined up on the base at Phu Bai, South Vietnam.

I also heard about individual soldiers in the field seeking similar revenge for a perceived grievance by deliberately shooting a member of their own unit. Such an incident would usually take place during the chaotic action of a firefight with the enemy where potential witnesses would understandably be concerned about their own well-being and not worrying about or noticing what others in their group did.

Such tragic incidents may have contributed to the decision at our base camp to lock up each of our assigned weapons, usually M-16 rifles, in a secure location so they would be unavailable to us unless our superiors deemed us in immediate danger. During the three or four occasions when the enemy lobbed mortar rounds into our base, we received orders to go into the heavily sandbagged bunkers for protection with no weapons issued. However, one night when we heard that sappers were attempting to breach our perimeter defenses and may have already done so, our commanders quickly issued us the M-16s from a nearby locked location so we could defend ourselves. Fortunately, we did not have to use our weapons that night, and I never did learn if the enemy successfully got through our perimeter defenses.

Despite the many challenges of life and threats to our survival at Phu Bai, I found compensations. For example, the base housed one of the most wonderful hamburger joints I have ever found not only in the military but also back in the States. How it got there and who was responsible for running it has always mystified me a bit. It may have been just an extension of the regular mess-hall system on the base. I never asked, and the subject never came up. I do know that it meant a bit of a hike to get to from my company's area, but man, absolutely worth the trip.

I don't remember how I first stumbled upon the little, barely marked shack way over in another part of the camp, but the hamburgers out of that place tasted so delicious that I visited it as often as I could. Something about the welcoming atmosphere created by fellow soldiers who worked at the shack's little front counter made the long hike totally worth it, too. Damn, I can almost taste those big and juicy burgers now.

I visited the chaplain's office on that base, too, although only once and with a completely opposite result. I went there because, despite my relief at carrying out my overseas tour of duty at a base camp instead of out in the boonies, the severe and constant demands of my first sergeant, Top, completely stressed me out. Yes, even a typing job in a war zone has its down sides.

Every day I worked for him—and, as I mentioned earlier, that was seven days a week for months on end—the first sergeant demanded I make absolutely no mistakes

Top, the irascible and unpredictable first sergeant of Headquarters Company, stressed me out.

when I typed a formal document or official document. If I happened to make a single typo as I worked on, for example, a common Article 13 (a document that presented a case against a particular soldier for committing any number of minor infractions), he would order me to redo the entire page. I had stacks of those Article 13s to type, so having to redo a whole page would invariably set me way back in production.

How about using Wite-Out to cover up the problem? Absolutely forbidden. And the basic typewriter the Army issued me didn't have the self-erase option of modern typewriters nor the easy delete button of everyday computers. My work as a company clerk probably would have been much easier in this new technological age.

If you have ever typed a letter or document, try doing it over and over again without making a single mistake. It's not like the computer era when you can push the delete key and forever erase your mistakes and then correct them. Top didn't single me out for intimidation, and all of us in his office felt the same fears. Having to produce perfectly typed documents may sound insignificant, but with me over an extended period of time, the stress I felt became almost unbearable. Still, I felt I had no alternative but to keep trying to meet the impossible standards set for me by the first sergeant.

I honestly feared that, if I expressed my displeasure to him, I would be sent out to the field, especially since my training designated me as an infantryman and not a clerk typist. I especially knew my precarious position as far as possibly being ordered out to the boonies as a specialist in indirect fire because a directive had already come from base command that all servicemen at the camp who had not served at least six months in the field would immediately be assigned to a field unit.

Command issued the directive after my several months in the Phu Bai camp, and when I heard it, my heart sank. I figured my luck had run out. But I never heard anything more about that order. As far as I know, no one carried it out. Maybe the higher-ups in my company successfully argued they needed me to keep the headquarters company operating effectively. I will never know why I never heard more about that directive, but the realization that I might be in the boonies at any time cast a shadow over my head and contributed greatly to the tension increasingly building up within me.

I became so conflicted about my participation in the war that at one point I even made a half-hearted attempt to be declared a conscientious objector. I met with an officer about it, but it looks like he never followed up on my request because I never heard back from him about it nor was I contacted about it by anyone else. Also, I was not sufficiently convinced within myself about the correctness of such a radical move that I ever pursued the issue. However, my head became so messed up that I finally decided to try to talk to the chaplain on the base. My gut told me that I couldn't talk honestly, candidly, and confidentially to anyone else on that base camp about the overwhelming stress I felt.

I managed to find some free time to take the long walk over to the chaplain's office. What happened there just blew my already messed-up mind. I nervously knocked on the door and felt tremendously relieved when the chaplain soon appeared. I asked him if I could please talk with him for a few minutes. I assumed he could see my distress.

His response? "You know, this is not a good time for that. I am trying to put together my sermon for the next service. Perhaps we can do it some other time?"

I was completely stunned. I stared at the middle-aged man a generation older than me. Dressed informally in neither military nor clerical clothing, he stood in front of me in the doorway. It was just the two of us there—no one else around. He didn't even invite me into his office.

It had taken just about every bit of my remaining emotional strength to put myself in the position of finally sharing my anxieties with someone I felt would understand

and whom I could trust. And that person chose to put the importance of the words he would say in an upcoming sermon over meeting with an actual living and breathing soldier to hear what he wanted to share.

I turned, walked away, and never went back.

That supposed man of God should never have been in that position, especially on an overseas base in a war zone where tensions and emotions run sky high and healthy outlets for those tensions and emotions are few and far between. I remember feeling extreme disappointment and disillusionment about what happened that day. So much for choosing humanity over words. And that from a chaplain, for crying out loud.

That same chaplain may have had misgivings about his decision later, because a month or so after my aborted meeting with him, he showed up in my headquarters' office and acknowledged my presence but said nothing more. Frankly, I could not have cared less to see the man again and made no overture to him in return.

At some point in my fourteen months of duty in that northern area of South Vietnam, my sergeant asked me if I would accompany him as his gunner in the Jeep to the old capital city of Hue. Our mission: to pick up his laundry.

An orphanage in that famous war-torn city made a few bucks seconding as a laundry business. My sergeant always wanted to look good, so he brought his

A bridge led to the heavily fortified, walled city of Hue, the old capital of Vietnam.

An old fortification stood near Hue.

We drove by the walled city of Hue.

Rows and rows of South Vietnamese houseboats lined up on a river between our base and Hue.

uniforms there regularly for laundering. Since our drive took place during daylight hours, we assumed it meant little personal risk to us. Also, it made me glad to get the chance to get the hell off the base for a while.

 Once our vehicle left base confines, it felt like a different world. Nestled against a backdrop of tall mountains, the Vietnamese countryside we drove through, if it weren't such a tragic war zone, could be described as spectacularly beautiful with many shades of tropical green filled with rice paddies and lush fields. Many rice farmers used teams of oxen to till wet ground, and the sight of those large, rugged animals in the fields added to the overall, intriguing beauty of that area for a Westerner such as me. Buddhist religious sites and monuments honoring the dead were common along the sides of the road we traveled.

 When we reached the outskirts of the former capital, a huge ancient wall came into view surrounding the city, thus giving Hue its sobriquet: The Walled City. As we drove closer to that wall, I couldn't help but notice its many pockmarks and blast scars resulting from fierce fighting there during the Tet lunar new year in 1968. Viet Cong and North Vietnamese forces eventually overwhelmed South Vietnamese soldiers defending the city during what came to be called the Tet Offensive. They rampaged through for days afterwards, in strikingly brutal fashion and with abandon, killing many of the leaders and intelligentsia who lived and worked there.

It took weeks of heavy fighting for South Vietnamese and US troops to take back that old capital. That battle and others during the Tet Offensive, seen live and in graphic detail on millions of TVs in the United States and elsewhere, undoubtedly added fuel to the fires of growing anti-war sentiment around the world. Over the years, the battle for Hue became a famous symbol of a tragic war that maybe American servicemen should not have been involved in in such a direct, deadly, and monumental way.

Certainly the Tet offensive monumentally scarred the ancient city of Hue after that Tet holiday turned into carnage and chaos. However, when I saw it two years later with my sergeant, it had fortunately recovered many of the features of a vibrant city. I found it truly refreshing to see the many children of the orphanage running around in playful fashion when we arrived to get Top's laundry. I took it as a sign that the city of Hue had begun to return to normal even while seemingly endless war engulfed the country. I felt relief at getting back to Phu Bai later that day but also was very glad I had been able to soak in the sights and sounds of the historic old capital area of Vietnam.

Troops in Phu Bai not able to go beyond the barbed wire perimeter of the camp, a fact for many of them, discovered a special place on the base where they could leave their worries behind and reenergize themselves. That establishment: the camp's Massage & Steam Bath, located, fortunately for us members of Headquarters' Company, 2nd Brigade, a short distance away from our area. As with the out-of-the-way little base hamburger stand, I don't know what unit of the US Army set up and operated such a facility. But there it was.

You could, for a nominal fee, use its facilities to get yourself a steam bath or, for a little more expensive fee, partake of the talents of one of the young Vietnamese women there to have a relaxing massage in the privacy of your own little room, if you could call it a room. It was big enough to have a massage table, the masseuse, and you, and that's about it. But hey, who's complaining? You lived in a war zone, supposedly defending the country from being overtaken by enemy forces, and you still had the opportunity for a nice steam bath and massage. A bit bizarre, perhaps, but not at all bad.

What was bad, however, was the chance of getting scalded to death using the steam baths. I remember entering this tiny cubicle surrounded by wooden walls on my left and right sides and behind me was a fully exposed large and incredibly hot pipe just inches back from the bench that I had to sit on. The only source of steam for about a dozen of the little booths with the wooden benches, that exposed pipe extended along the entire wall of the room. Maybe you could rightly classify me as a bit of a worrier, but I could in no way enjoy a relaxing steam bath when that damned pipe filled with boiling hot water looked like it could spring a leak at any moment or worse, just blow to smithereens. In fact, the whole steam bath area looked like rank amateur carpenters and plumbers constructed it with not a whole lot of thought put into making it safe for customers. There, as occurs so often in life, the fantasy of having a nice steam bath promised far more than the available reality in that camp. At best, you might give it a try once or twice, but more could constitute a suicidal act.

Three of my buddies waited in front of the (in)famous Steam Bath and Massage Parlor at our base camp.

Interestingly enough, that same disappointing experience duplicated itself in the building's other attractive offering, namely the massage service. In a vulgar and base kind of way, I guess you could say that the facility gave you what you came there for, which in probably every case meant more than just receipt of a standard massage. The service provided you there did quiet your internal testosterone battles for a few hours for a relatively small sum of money. But, if you really wanted to do anything more than that with the innocent young maiden (NOT!) attending to you, then you somehow (translated: You gave her a helluva lot more money) had to convince that fair maiden that the wad of cash you just handed to her compensated for the risk to her of immediately losing her job if caught in the act.

Basically, if you opted for anything more than a special massage in that joint, you would undoubtedly blow this month's pay and probably next month's, too, in the process. In other words, what you got in there didn't come close to what you paid for getting it. So again, any visit to that base camp facility for a massage after your first or second visit added up to, in my humble opinion, a very foolish waste of your time and money.

Those of us in headquarters' company did have contact daily with young Vietnamese women, but they provided service and talents of a very different sort than those offered by the young ladies of the Massage & Steam Bath. The so-called hooch girls came through the base's security checkpoints every day to keep our living quarters in reasonable shape. I think two women were assigned to each hooch. Considering that each hooch contained from six to eight young, healthy males who had little or no physical contact with females for months on end, the guys treated the hooch girls with admirable respect as they cleaned day after day. I can't remember a single instance of a problem between those young women and the troops on the base, and since I worked in the headquarters' office, I think that I would have heard of any problems if they existed.

In addition, every day the male counterparts to hooch girls arrived on the base. They provided yet another very different service for us. They cleaned out the many latrines on the base. Then they dumped all the solid waste into giant metal drums and set it all on fire. Even now I can almost smell the stench permeating the camp from those drums of burning human waste, but believe me, it is not an aroma you would want to recall in any way fondly. Somehow, after exposure to that very unpleasant smell for weeks and months at a time, everyone seemed to get used to it and for the most part acted like it didn't exist. Because that smell mixed with so many other strong smells, some pleasant, some not, in the air that we breathed in South Vietnam, we could deny the assault to our olfactory organs. The extremely hot, humid air in that tropical country seemed to hold and accentuate every fragrance, smell, and odor produced from natural fruits and vegetables farmed and cooked, animals both semi-wild and domesticated, flowering plants, and yes, some unsanitary conditions within its borders, so the oppressive and awful smell of burning human waste constituted just one of many different odors that troops dealt with during their tour of duty in South Vietnam. In the end, it was all part of the overall experience of being over there.

We Westerners all had to adjust to another different scene while stationed in that Southeast Asian country: monsoon season. Torrential rain literally fell for hours at a time every day over a period of months and turned dirt roads, paths, and open ground into quagmires of deep, thick mud. To be out on patrol in the boonies during that time must have made it a thousand times more difficult and dreadful for the troops. Even back in base camp where I luckily called home, monsoon season comprised one of those miserable situations you just had to get through to complete your tour of duty.

Fortunately, in consideration of monsoons, the military had built all camp buildings on stilts. When you left your hooch to go to work, to the latrine or shower room, to eat at the mess hall, or even to visit a friend in another hooch, during those months of non-stop heavy rain, you needed to follow wooden or metal boardwalks that the Army engineers constructed to keep you from sinking into knee-deep mud always just inches away from your boots. Of course, sometimes with no boardwalk in the direction you headed, not only did your feet and boots get totally muddied up, but you also muddied up your hooch when you returned later. I am sure the hooch girls hated the onset of monsoon season because it made their work much, much harder. I imagine, too, that constant rain made their daily trip to our base camp in the morning and their return to their nearby villages later in the day just a miserable situation for them. I wonder how conquering Viet Cong and North Vietnamese treated them, along with all other villagers in the area who worked at our base camp during that war, a few years later when US troops pulled out and the South Vietnamese surrendered to the North Vietnamese. Did the conquerors ostracize or physically abuse them or their family members for helping the enemy? Unfortunately, I imagine it happened in far too many cases.

A Vietnamese man took charge of the hooch girls from nearby villages as they lined up on base.

Two Vietnamese women took responsibility for cleaning our hooch.

I have already mentioned the horrifying situation at the base brought on by fraggings. Another real problem among some troops involved their use of illicit drugs in camp. Except for using marijuana and hashish, fairly common among soldiers I lived and worked with, others used much more potent and devastating drugs like heroin and other opium-based compounds under the radar. I imagine supportive personnel stationed near headquarters rarely used more potent and risky drugs, but I learned later of serious drug use among some soldiers out patrolling and fighting in the field. A few users, I am sure, felt the need to get relief of any kind from the incredible and constant stress that they underwent as they patrolled in heavily forested and mountainous areas outside the relative safety of the base camp.

Despite the real risk of overdosing or becoming addicted to their drug of choice, I am sure some guys decided the high and temporary escape from their troubles justified the risk. Then, too, maybe some users already had a habit from before their time in the military, and because of apparently easy access to high potency drugs such as heroin in South Vietnam, those soldiers continued their dangerous practice for fun, profit, or both. I imagine it as undoubtedly one of very few ways for a soldier to make extra money while stationed overseas.

To be faithful to a full disclosure policy, I must say that I indulged in some pot smoking on the base perhaps a half dozen times during my overseas tour of duty. I remember one time when a buddy and I climbed up an abandoned guard tower in the camp and smoked some really good hashish, a stronger form of marijuana very popular and available in Vietnam. We enjoyed our smoke in the relative privacy of the security shack about thirty feet off the ground. After a pleasant time up there, we proceeded to float around our headquarters' area for a while while high on that stuff.

As we entered the little informal library of paperback books for our company personnel, I felt as if everybody in there looked at me kind of funny, like they knew I was high and walking about three feet off the ground. But in my mellow condition, I didn't give a damn and proceeded on my merry way. Unlike some of my buddies

I strummed a guitar, top, during one of my lighter moments in the Phu Bai base camp. Jim, left; John, right; and I lined up in the hooch area of our base.

in the company, I never really got into the marijuana or hashish scene in a big way. I wouldn't have even known where to go or who to talk to if I wanted to experiment with opium-based drugs available clandestinely on the base.

I mentioned earlier that twice during my service in South Vietnam I neglected to think of real risk and danger in a very active war zone and instead saw opportunity for an adventurous experience. Well, please allow me tell you now about one of those times. I had a promotion from Specialist, E-4, to Sergeant, E-5 (that turned out to be a mini-adventure too, and I will tell you why shortly). My superiors had officially designated me the company clerk of Headquarters' 2nd Brigade. Occasionally a guy from US Army's intelligence division came into the headquarters office, and I always found him fun to talk with.

I soon learned that part of his job involved convincing the Viet Cong in our northern section of the country to surrender and turn over their weapons in exchange for receiving amnesty from the South Vietnamese government. As part of the deal, the government would give each a plot of ground deemed suitable for farming. In order to get out the word about the amnesty program to Viet Cong living and fighting in northern fields and mountains, my friend flew a helicopter to areas considered heavily populated with the enemy. Then, as his copter hovered just a few feet above the treetops, he dropped thousands of what were called chu hoi leaflets to enemy troops thought to be hiding there. Translated from Vietnamese, chu hoi meant, roughly, "surrender, and we will protect and provide for you."

The more I talked with the intelligence officer about his activity, the more intrigued I became. One day I suggested that I would I like to accompany him on one of his chu hoi helicopter flights. He agreed. I would help him drop the leaflets from our copter to the enemy below.

It wasn't long before we set a date to meet at one of the camp's helicopter pads. I looked forward to that day with great enthusiasm. When it arrived, the officer quickly ushered me into a small Huey helicopter, showed me where to sit and how to strap myself in, and handed me a box of the leaflets I would toss out of the copter as we arrived at a designated spot. In all, four servicemen flew in that helicopter: the pilot, the intelligence officer, a gunner who would fire a mounted machine gun in the event we came under enemy fire, and me.

Upon taking off, we headed straight for battle-scarred open countryside miles away from the base camp and soon flew over rice paddies, winding rivers, and tilled

Here's what I saw from the helicopter as I took part in a chu hoi mission.

farmland. Eventually, we saw a region of thick forest that would provide a natural hiding place for enemy forces. Within a few minutes, we began to descend and prepare to drop thousands of chu hoi leaflets to the reported enemy below.

Our pilot dropped the helicopter lower and lower until we hovered just over the treetops. At that moment, it dawned on me that, without thinking clearly about the consequences, I had voluntarily put myself in the middle of a potentially very dangerous situation. It was a sobering and very forbidding feeling to realize we were essentially alone out there with no close backup as we offered any enemy combatants below a practically stationary target to shoot out of the sky.

As a necessary part of our mission, we had deliberately put ourselves in an area believed to harbor lethal enemy forces. Our copter easily flew within range of a round from an AK-47 rifle, the standard and highly effective Viet Cong weapon, let alone a projectile from a shoulder-launched rocket or one of their powerful machine guns. For the other three guys in the cockpit with me, it was their job in the military and they didn't have much choice in the matter. However, in my case, I had volunteered for the darned thing, thinking I would find it a much more interesting thing to do than typing some damned document.

Well, it was interesting all right, but right then it seemed a foolishly risky endeavor that could at any moment turn catastrophic. As our small copter hovered over one area of that forest below, the intelligence officer and I tossed out handfuls and handfuls of the leaflets. The more that we did it, the more that I kicked myself for allowing my sense of adventure to blind me temporarily to the fact that we were in a real war with real people wanting us dead or captured. Then, it certainly didn't seem like much of an adventure any more. In fact, it felt more like a very precarious situation that I wanted to escape from as fast as possible.

Thankfully, the Fates were especially kind to the crew and me that day. As we watched leaflets slowly floating and fluttering down through the air to the trees below, the pilot in that tiny helicopter headed us back to the relative safety and security of our base camp in Phu Bai. I was one relieved and happy soldier when my feet touched the ground inside of our base. I realized very clearly that, while I appreciated the experience and had fortunately once again dodged a bullet, I recognized how lucky I had been. I made no attempt to do it again.

And now my story about being promoted from Specialist, E-4 to Sergeant, E-5. Back in my headquarters office one day, I heard they needed me in the building

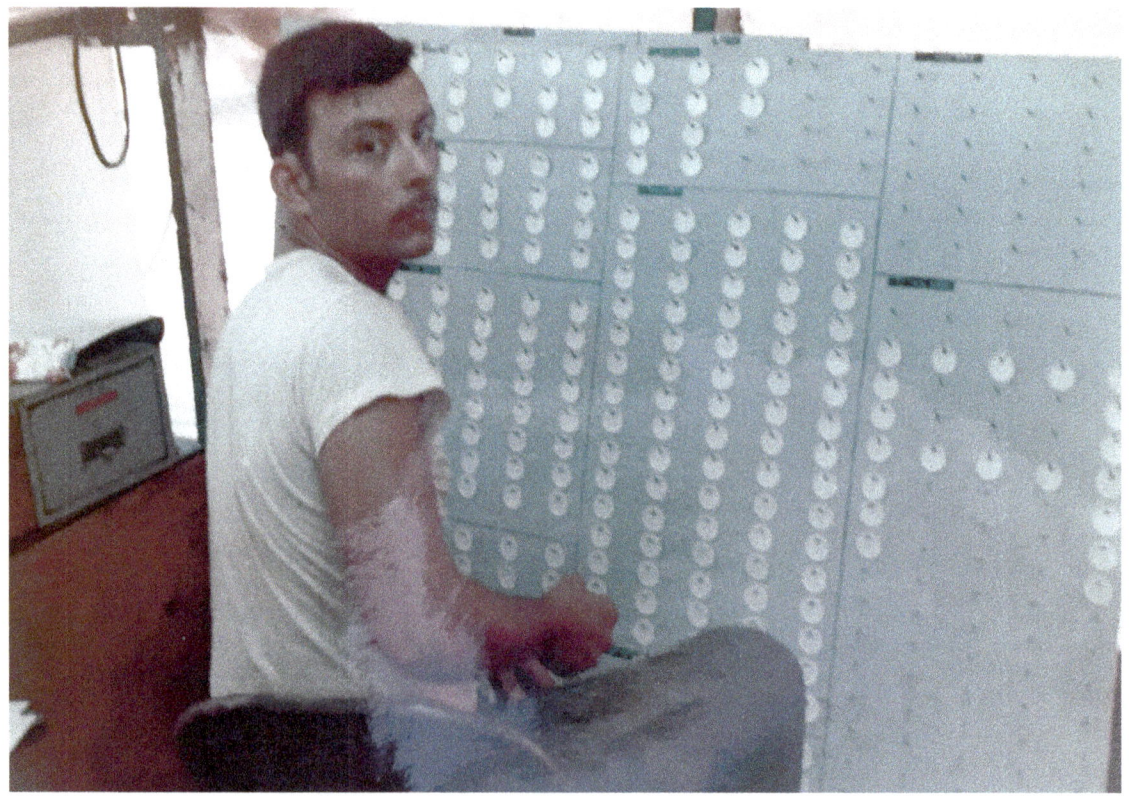

My assistant, Jerry George, in the headquarters office checked the board to make sure we could account for every soldier in our company.

next to us. I didn't know why, but following orders, I went over there to see what was up. Upon entering the barracks, I noticed officers from our company who asked me to sit in a chair facing them. I still had no idea why I was there, and it definitely would have been helpful if I had known. In the Army, a lot of strange and unforeseen things can happen to you, so it could have turned out to be any number of things, some good, some not so good. They asked me a series of questions about proper military behavior. One particular I remember involved what I would view as more important in a combat mission, namely, securing the safety of fellow soldiers or successfully completing the mission my unit had been ordered to carry out.

As I tried to answer questions like that as well as I could, a dog (yes, a dog) came to me seemingly out of nowhere and wanted me to pat its head. Here I was (and I still didn't know this comprised the official interview for promotion to sergeant) in a fairly formal setting arranged by the officers in front of me, and I had to figure out quickly what to do with the friendly but strange dog at my side. I responded by reaching over and petting the dog as I answered one of the officers' questions. Little did I know that paying attention to the dog posed a big problem to at least one of the officers there.

In my opinion, the whole bizarre setting reflected poorly on those responsible for setting it up. I got called into a formal interview without notice nor being told what the interview was about. Then during that interview by soldiers of much higher rank than me, out of the blue a dog sauntered over and wanted me to pet him. What the hell was the dog doing there in the first place? And what difference did it make if I petted the dog or not as I answered a question? The dog's presence hadn't distracted me from focusing on answering the question, so why the big deal? But apparently it was a big deal to one of the interviewing officers who worked in the headquarters office, because when I returned to my regular desk there later, he threw a mini tantrum about it.

Despite the unpleasantness of the "Pooch in the Hooch" incident, I learned a few days later that I had been promoted to Sergeant, E-5. As you will see, being awarded that higher rank turned out to be my entry pass to some more unusual and unforgettable experiences during my tour in South Vietnam.

When a soldier reaches the rank of sergeant, he or she has more responsibility but also receives more pay along with extra benefits. For example, I supposedly deserved increased respect from my fellow soldiers now that I had an E-5 classification, but I don't know how to prove or disprove that. I could, though, eat meals in a special mess hall for soldiers of E-5 rank or higher. I found that the food provided in that mess hall of very good quality and well prepared, but I really had no complaints about the quality of the food I had been served in the mess hall for lower-ranked soldiers. From my point of view, eating in a different mess hall amounted to more of a social-status thing than an upgrade in the food served.

The bigger privilege, in my opinion, meant access to on-base entertainment not available to any soldier with a lower ranking than E-5. What kind of entertainment, do you ask? Well, a live music affair I attended on base in my new role and rank as sergeant provides a striking example. As I entered the huge tent set up for that purpose, I quickly discovered I attended not just any ol' live music concert.

Not surprisingly, seating appeared ordered by rank with the first couple of rows filled by top officers. They, of course, had a better view of the band, all four of them female, standing on the stage. All were young, quite attractive, and apparently of Vietnamese nationality. As the band performed, it quickly became apparent that one would rate this concert XXX.

Why would I put the performance in such an extremely risqué category?

Well, I quickly came to the conclusion when suddenly all four members of the band began disrobing and started doing some unseemly things with smoke from a cigarette borrowed from one of the officers in the audience.

It soon became apparent that the young women all displayed a remarkable ability to control their so-called private parts to the point that those parts both inhaled cigarette smoke into their lower body and, a few moments later, those same special parts exhaled smoke in a series of short and controlled puffs. Quite an eye-catching and amazing talent, really.

And then, as the four naked females gyrated and displayed their remarkable talents, musical and otherwise, to the appreciative and enthusiastic crowd, one of them exited the stage and approached those sitting in the front row.

And that's when I discovered that another unannounced privilege awaited the highest-ranking officer present. The completely naked young entertainer jumped on the lap of that officer and probably turned up his blood pressure and other vitals by a good thirty percent. If finding himself in this rather unusual public position bothered the officer, I saw no sign of it. In fact, he looked like he enjoyed the hell out of whatever the young woman was doing on his lap.

I decided it was time to leave that tent filled with raucous revelers and return in one piece to my company area. I say that because I began to think that such a big gathering of high ranking soldiers would unfortunately be an ideal time and place for a fragging to take place, that is, for a soldier with revenge on his mind to roll a live grenade into that tent filled with officers and non-coms. With even a slight chance of such a thing occurring, I did not want to be around if it did.

Have I mentioned how important cigarettes and the f-word were to surviving a tour of duty in South Vietnam? No, I probably haven't, because one does not generally refer to either in a positive or praiseworthy way. But at least in my case, I don't know if I could have made it through a total of fourteen months in that war-torn country without the release from general tension that the two of them provided me: namely, my generous use of the f-word in any informal conversation coupled with a long, satisfying draw on a filter cigarette.

Months after my honorable discharge from the US Army, a buddy of mine in the States pointed out to me that I used the f-word surprisingly often whenever I spoke. And I smoked cigarettes a helluva lot, too. Beginning with Day One in basic training and right until that wonderful United Airlines plane flew me back to the States and freedom nineteen months later, cigarettes and the f-word served as my constant companions. They provided crutches that steadied me when I felt like I might lose it. I don't regret using them at all back then, even though I have since completely stopped smoking and using the (in)famous f-word much more judiciously.

The benefit of going on one in-country rest and recreation, or R&R, and at least two regular R&Rs outside of the country boosted morale for us overseas soldiers. All the troops looked forward with great enthusiasm to R&R, especially out-of-country trips. When I served in South Vietnam in 1970 and 1971, each soldier could choose among Thailand, Hawaii, Hong Kong, and Australia for his two one-week out-of-country vacations. I think that you would agree on the attractiveness of all those destinations.

Because I ended up staying an additional two months in Vietnam after completing my regular twelve-month tour, I received a third R&R paid for and arranged by Uncle Sam. And due to the incredibly great time I had when I went to Hong Kong for my first R&R, I went back a second time to enjoy another week with a special female friend who lived and worked in that really spectacular city.

One of my buddies from advanced infantry training back in Fort Lewis, with whom I stayed in touch by in-country mail also deployed to South Vietnam. He met me in Hong Kong for the first R&R but chose to spend a week in Thailand for his second. His choice did not disappoint him. And after my attempt to accompany him to Thailand fell through, my decision to go back to Hong Kong for another seven days and nights of temporary freedom didn't disappoint me. Both places turned out to be fabulous stops for US servicemen, especially those who faced daily horrors of life as combatants in the field and who felt they had nothing to lose.

Being on R&R meant an opportunity for a soldier to set aside his troubles and fears for a week and enjoy his time like there was no tomorrow. Tragically, for those soldiers engaged in frequent combat in South Vietnam, too often there was no tomorrow after they returned to infantry units in the rice paddies, jungles, and mountains of that besieged country.

Hong Kong was a city of contrasts with modern US warships moored in the spectacular harbor alongside age-old Asian junks and sampans. Entire families lived in those traditional vessels of ancient origin, while on land rows and rows of glistening skyscrapers towered high above areas of extreme poverty and deprivation. The city fascinated me from the moment I stepped off the plane, and fortunately I got to see some of its more intriguing features before I returned to my base camp in South Vietnam.

My US Army buddy Michael and I quickly hailed a taxi at the airport. On the way to our hotel, the taxi driver dropped us off at one of the city's famed tailor shops. In a surprisingly short time, the tailor measured and fitted me for a brand new suit at what seemed a bargain price. Apparently the taxi driver and tailor shop had a good arrangement going. Even though Michael and I hadn't asked the driver to stop at the tailor shop on our long awaited R&R, we had no inclination to complain about the little side-trip.

Soon after, we arrived at our hotel, checked in, and left to explore bustling city streets filled with cars, motorbikes, rickshaws, and pedestrians. Not surprisingly and completely by chance, we ended up at a bar called The 007, where we not only quenched our thirst but also satisfied our need for female companionship. Two young and attractive bar girls approached us. Soon, they bid goodbye to their beloved female boss, whom they referred to as Mama San, and left with us.

Mama San watched over her girls in the bar and also kept track of them 24/7 wherever they went with their military friends. Basically, she was the Asian equivalent of a brothel's madam back in the States, and the women who worked for her seemed to have great respect and affection for her.

My new companion for the week, Sandy, turned out to be a both physical and emotional pleasure. And Michael enjoyed his new temporary friend, too. The four of us spent the next few days and nights together, eating at some of Hong Kong's many good restaurants, going bowling and sightseeing, and, of course, partying until late at night in our hotel.

We had a blast all week with one exception. Unexpectedly, my friend Michael got both of us into a bit of a jam one night back at the 007 while we socialized with the ladies there. Suddenly, Michael became upset about something, and he and a bar girl got into a heated argument. Immediately Mama San intervened, and it appeared that she would call the police and have them come to the bar.

My dear friend, Sandy, waited in front of a flower store in Hong Kong, top. Cool me enjoyed the sights and sounds of Hong Kong during R and R.

A huge restaurant floated in Victoria Harbour, Hong Kong, top.
A multitude of fishing boats moored in Victoria Harbour, Hong Kong.

I wanted out of that situation as quickly as possible, but Michael didn't want to call the incident over. He and Mama San kept arguing over what had happened. I envisioned Michael and me held and interrogated by the US military police in the city, and I most assuredly wanted none of that.

Within a few harrowing minutes, at least for me, I somehow coaxed my buddy out of the bar, and we escaped down the city's busy streets before any law enforcement personnel arrived. That incident was the only unpleasant time of an otherwise great week in Hong Kong, though. Later, we happily rejoined Sandy and Michael's girlfriend, and the rest of the night went very well. But, frankly, after my plans for R and R in Bangkok didn't work out, my destination of choice for that second R&R period rested more on the young woman named Sandy, with whom I had spent an unforgettable few days not too many weeks earlier.

Sandy and I had kept in touch by mail since my first stay in Hong Kong, and clearly we had enjoyed each other's company. She wrote that she really wanted to see me again and encouraged me to bring a friend along next time so he could hook up with Marie, a special friend of hers at the bar. Sandy wanted the four of us to enjoy the week together.

It wasn't hard for me to say yes to that arrangement proposed by my new friend in Hong Kong, and a couple of months later I found myself stepping off a plane once again in that exciting city. Two US Army acquaintances, Jack and Steve, accompanied me to our hotel. Then Jack and I headed off to my old haunt, the 007 Bar, while Steve, who apparently was gay, searched out his own pleasures. Upon arriving at the 007, it really bummed me out to learn that Sandy had other client commitments until halfway through my R&R week.

Disappointing, yes, but not to the point that I would spend the first three days and nights of my week's vacation pouting and letting it all slip away. No way, José. I turned my attention to whoever approached me at the bar and enjoyed the company of those working women until I could be with Sandy again.

That day eventually arrived, and Sandy enthusiastically showed me parts of Hong Kong she thought I would like to see. She led me on a hike way up a hill on the outskirts of the city that resulted in a fantastic view of the harbor. Maritime vessels of all kinds, shapes, and ages filled the shining waters as far as you could see. It was a really impressive sight, one that has stayed with me through the years.

Toward the end of our stay together, Sandy brought me to one of her favorite local Chinese-style restaurants, tried unsuccessfully to teach me how to use chopsticks, and then presented me with a new set of chopsticks as a reminder of our good times together. At our final farewell, she surprised me with a gift of men's jewelry and an Asian style bathrobe before we said our goodbyes. I was really impressed by her generosity and sensitivity. She remained a friend-by-mail for months after that. Sandy was a special person to me, and I will never forget her.

A decidedly different animal, my in-country mini-vacation of three days and nights took place at a 101st Airborne Division-only location on the shore of the South China Sea. Devoid of signs of a brutal wartime conflict that many soldiers had just left literally hours before, it offered us live music, plenty of food and drink, and a refreshing relaxed atmosphere.

That was such a weird thing about that war. In an age of high-speed transportation, soldiers involved in heavy combat one day found themselves at a welcoming mini-resort complete with sandy beaches and music concerts the next day, all within the same country. I doubt that infantry troops in World War I, World War II, or the Korean War experienced anything like it.

How do you wrap your head around a situation that engages you in fierce combat one day and has you partying at a beach the next? And then three days later you are again worried about stepping on a land mine or setting off a booby-trap that would blow both your legs off? It was, and still is, asking possibly too much of a soldier to maintain a healthy mind as well as a sense of humanity through a series of experiences like that.

One memory I have of being at the in-country R&R facility amounted to a big turn-off for me. I have always liked to go fishing, so when I learned I could hire the services of a Vietnamese fishing guide at the facility, I jumped at the chance. Upon meeting my designated guide, I got in the back of his small sampan, and he headed us to a nearby estuary that I hoped would be filled with hungry fish. The supposed fishing guide looked, unfortunately, like a local teenager who knew how to drive a primitive sampan to and from the camp. As far as I could tell, that summed up his prowess as a fishing guide.

The young man spoke even less English than I spoke Vietnamese, so right there that severely limited our ability to communicate with each other. To make matters worse, he acted incredibly bored with the whole exercise and appeared totally uninterested in providing me with any kind of positive fishing experience. As I cast a line from the back of his sampan, he sat as far in the front as possible, continually smoked the local example of what we would call a cigarette, and just stared out over the water.

Of course, I never came close to catching anything in the approximately three hours we were out there, and when my agreed-upon hours on the water were up, the young man laconically and mechanically drove the craft slowly back to camp. My guide got paid something for his services, or in reality lack of services, but otherwise it was a complete waste of time for both of us.

So beware. If you happen to travel overseas and engage the services of a supposed local "professional" as part of the attractive amenities offered by the hotel where you stay (and in this case I don't mean any service of the X-rated kind, although a similar warning would certainly apply to them, too), it behooves you to check out the reputation and professionalism of that kind of specialist before you fork over your hard-earned money to that individual.

My supposed fishing guide during my in-country R and R really didn't show any interest in helping me find fish.

Vietnamese residences lined the shore and boats worked the sea near Eagle Beach, site of our in-country R and R.

Eagle Beach on the South China Sea provided the location for our in-country R and R.

I mention this unpleasant episode to you for another reason, too, because it demonstrates how unreal the Vietnam experience could turn out for American and other allied troops deployed there. To me, the experience exemplifies how challenging it was for Americans or the allied troops involved in active combat situations to allow themselves to live in and appreciate the new culture where they found themselves. I would imagine that it would be especially hard for soldiers coming out of combat to have enough time to process successfully where they were on a particular day, what they were supposed to be doing, and why they were doing it from one day to the next.

Going on a bizarre fishing trip one day and then fearing for your life the following day while engaging in a firefight with unseen enemy forces would be just one small example. I acknowledge that a soldier in combat should be given an opportunity to rest and recover away from the field of battle, but I am not convinced that a quick ride to a mini-resort is the best way to do it.

A feeling of dis-connect is not a pleasant feeling, nor is it helpful, for a human being in any situation. But, in my opinion, servicemen of all stripes in that war-torn country in Southeast Asia experienced it on far too many occasions and then turned to drugs and alcohol to alleviate the pain, confusion, and emptiness they felt inside.

My first R&R was completely different in many ways from the two R&Rs to Hong Kong that followed, both in location and very definitely in content. I asked a girlfriend from the States to meet me in Hawaii for my first week of temporary freedom, and by the end of that week, we were engaged to be married. I even bought her a lovely diamond ring to prove it. What can I say, other than I was impulsive and immature and didn't realize the consequences of what I had done until several weeks after I had returned to South Vietnam?

Of course, after I regretted what I had done, I wanted to break off the relationship, a task made somewhat easier for me because I was thousands of miles away. Part of me knew I had made a huge and insensitive mistake not at all fair to the young woman who had agreed to marry me. I take no pride in what I did but felt at the time that I had no other alternative but to end the engagement. Young, impetuous, and immature—those words describe what led me to bring about such an unfortunate and emotionally painful situation.

How did she sneak into the base camp???

During Hawaiian R and R, I saw many volcanic mountains.

Of course, staying in touch with friends and family while a member of the military fulfilled his or her tour of duty crucially affected a soldier's mental and emotional health. In the early 1970s during my overseas tour, we communicated across miles and even oceans primarily by letter mail and, eventually, the telephone facilitated magnificently by volunteer ham radio operators.

Mail call at any military base camp in a faraway land constituted a hugely important part of a soldier's day, naturally including my base in Phu Bai. Fortunately, I received an abundance of letters from loved ones and friends. Hearing from those people regularly gave me a big emotional lift. How lonely and depressing it must have felt for fellow soldiers anxiously waiting to hear their names shouted out at the daily mail call instead to hear only other soldiers' names.

In a day before email and cell phone recordings, some of my dear friends sent cassette tapes they had recorded for me. And, of course, my fellow soldiers and I spent hours of free time responding to the wonderful letters of love and support. The US Post Office provided outstanding service for those of us deployed halfway across the globe. It must have been a herculean task for the people responsible for letters and packages so efficiently delivered to each soldier stationed throughout South Vietnam. My hat goes off to them.

Toward the end of my tour in Vietnam, another wonderful way to stay in touch with family and friends became available through a terrific global system set up by volunteer ham-radio operators. Those men and women worked together to coordinate and link calls made by overseas military personnel to loved ones in the States. It didn't matter what state the serviceman wanted to call. Their network of operators covered every state in the union.

If I recall correctly, the program limited each ham-operator-assisted phone call to three minutes. Either the caller or person on the receiving end had to say "Over" at the end of a sentence. I recall with great fondness talking with my Dad on one of those calls and laughing good-naturedly at our amateurish attempts to remember to use the word "Over" as we said our quick hellos and best wishes while passing along any big news. Soldiers in my unit, me included, lined up for hours at our company headquarters to spend three minutes on that ham phone with a special person thousands of miles away and worlds away. I never regretted waiting in those long lines to make the short call.

I have already told you about some of the more salacious entertainment available to us servicemen in South Vietnam, but I haven't yet described the remarkable event that took place when the legendary Bob Hope and his entourage came to our area. Believe me, it turned out that a whole lot of soldiers enjoyed the sights and sounds of his show. Military personnel from many units throughout the northern region of the country poured into grandstands set up in a field in front of a giant stage. The well-known Mr. Hope treated us to a tribute to the troops accompanied by the famous and incredibly attractive Ann-Margret and other entertainers Mr. Hope brought with him.

Bob Hope had his critics after being in the public eye for so many years, but I, for one, will always be a real fan of his because of the many trips he took overseas to entertain troops and provide them with a breather from the stresses of being in an active war zone. The appreciative crowd must have been in the thousands, and it didn't come as a big surprise when Ann-Margret received probably the most enthusiastic reception from the predominantly male crowd. I am very glad that I had the chance to attend such an unforgettable and legendary extravaganza while I was in the military.

US Army soldiers of the 101st Airborne Division headed to the grandstands for the Bob Hope Special.

Another memorable but decidedly more low-key event I attended during my tour took place right at my base camp in Phu Bai. I got a chance to go to a morning briefing by an officer covering the operations planned that day against enemy forces in our area. The briefing officer used a large map to pinpoint where our ground and air forces would try to engage the enemy over the next twenty-four hours. I found the meeting riveting.

The briefing gave me the opportunity a few hours later to make sense of the sights and sounds of a US Apache helicopter gunship pounding a suspected enemy position with rockets and missiles far off in mountains visible from our base. If that deadly barrage of explosives eliminated an enemy position on the mountainside, it may have prevented us from coming under sustained mortar attack that night.

No one took mortar attacks lightly. I remember hurrying inside one of the big sandbag bunkers in our company area one evening when the base's warning siren blared. I listened intently as mortar rounds were fired into our base camp. They landed closer and closer to my position. Mortar specialists "walked rounds in" to zero in on a target. The increasingly loud thronking sound made by the mortar round as it fired grabbed the immediate attention of those who realized the rounds dropped closer and closer to their defensive positions.

No matter how far from the stage, soldiers enjoyed the Bob Hope Special featuring Ann-Margret.

Fortunately, for those of us huddled inside a bunker that evening, the mortar fire ceased before it reached our area. We found the experience sobering, nonetheless. It meant, in fact, that at least some of the enemy lurked not far from the perimeter of our camp. We could not in any way justify complacency about maintaining proper security.

I would be amiss if I didn't mention how the word "short" assumed importance to each of the US military stationed in South Vietnam. I hadn't heard that word used in the States in context of how US troops commonly used it throughout that troubled country. In our military world, to be "short" meant you had very little time left in your overseas tour of duty. Soldiers coveted the position regardless if patrolling in the field or serving at one of the many base camps.

Most soldiers kept a "short calendar" in their living quarters, which consisted of a drawing of some kind of animal over empty numbered boxes. The number of boxes depended upon how many days the soldier had left in Vietnam before completing his tour of duty. I think the most common short calendars had a hundred numbered boxes, but some had sixty or even thirty. As a soldier completed each day over there, he colored in one box on his calendar. It may sound a little childish, but I'll tell you that marking off another day on your short calendar helped keep up morale and spirit.

One of my happiest days occurred when I learned nine or ten months into my tour of duty in South Vietnam that our headquarters' company would have a new top sergeant. First Sergeant DeLucia had driven me close to crazy with his outrageous work demands and unnerving tantrums in the office, but finally we learned of his reassignment to a post in South Korea. From my point of view, it was "Good riddance, Top." His departure could not have come soon enough for me.

To replace him, the US Army sent a man much more easily described as a good and reasonable human being. From Day One of the new first sergeant's arrival, my life in headquarters company improved considerably. I mentioned earlier that, from the first day of my assignment to the 101st Airborne Division, Top DeLucia expected us to work seven days a week, 365 days of the year. We did, with rare exceptions, and we did it without complaint. But right away, the new first sergeant told us we would each have one day off a week.

Man, we liked this guy a lot already when we heard that. Also, the new boss appeared to be pretty low-key. Yes, he expected us to complete our assigned work and do it well, but he did not cultivate the constant stressful atmosphere fostered by the former first sergeant. Common sense expectations became much more the theme of our workplace.

What a relief. The first sergeant approved my work as long as I took care of the most important responsibility for a company clerk, namely, accounting for every soldier in the unit each day. Of course, we had no computers back then. My assistant and I used a simple system of attaching a ring holding a paper tag labeled with a soldier's name to a hook on a bulletin board that matched the person's assigned work section for that day. Together, the labeled rings totaled the exact number of soldiers assigned to each section of the company. When a hook held a labeled ring, it showed which soldier filled which position.

As I mentioned earlier, the rest of my day in the office involved handling the many phone calls that came into headquarters company. I also had to stay up to date with typing the staff's correspondence and official documents. In the more comfortable work environment with a reasonable workload, my assistant and I often had a few moments each day in the office when we could socialize and relax a bit.

I enjoyed the more easygoing atmosphere in our unit after work hours ended, too. For example, the new Top welcomed us to join him in viewing some of the

I pointed out one of our obscene signs in camp

rather unusual but interesting private films that somehow he always managed to have in his possession. The films would undoubtedly fit into the Adults Only category. Hey, the guy was no saint, but neither was I or most of my fellow soldiers. Especially stuck in a damned war zone by Uncle Sam for all those many months, I didn't intend to be one either.

Remember how my *Have Racquet, Will Travel* mandate showed up in basic training when my instructor inquired about my tennis background? Well, incredibly, it showed up again in more remarkable form during my time at Phu Bai base camp.

Prior to my arrival at Phu Bai, the Army Corps of Engineers had constructed a full-size, concrete tennis court on the base. I mentioned the surprising existence of the tennis court in a letter to a friend, David Fowler, back in Connecticut. Lo and behold, I received a package later from him containing a tennis racquet and can of balls.

My friendship with Dave dated back to when he and I played tennis together at the Shore & Country Club. Once, we played doubles together there in a game I doubt either of us will ever forget. We both played "in the zone" that day. It seemed like every ball we hit was a winner, and we simply could not miss a shot if we tried. We qualified as absolutely unbeatable that day, and we definitely shared a few laughs over it later.

Some days, when we didn't play tennis, Dave invited me to go fishing for striped bass with him around the islands of Long Island Sound in his newly acquired boat. We always had a good time fishing and playing tennis.

By the time Dave sent me the tennis racquet, he already had built a tennis court in his backyard and used it professionally to give private lessons. *The New York Times* did an article about his unique and successful operation on his own property. I appreciated his gesture of friendship and that he went to the time and expense of providing me with equipment to play tennis at my base camp in South Vietnam.

When the package arrived one day at mail call, it was a very pleasant surprise. Of course, I had to try out my gift, so after work, I hiked over to the tennis court and hit a few balls to the imaginary player on the other side of the net. No one else I knew on base had the means or desire to play tennis, so that one visit to the court turned out to be my only sojourn into the world of tennis in the warzone area known as Phu Bai.

I definitely felt odd on that tennis court, hitting some balls around when, not far beyond our camp's barbed wire perimeter, a real war thundered on. The unanticipated experience provided another example of that surreal disconnect I mentioned earlier. And, as you will soon see, *Have Racquet, Will Travel* would unexpectedly continue to connect me to my past and to my future.

Well, the night finally arrived: the night before I would climb into a C-130 transport plane, strap myself in against its inside wall along with fifteen or twenty other soldiers whose tour of duty was up, and blissfully fly off to the huge Da Nang Air Base to the south for an eventual flight back to the States. That night, I celebrated and said goodbye to guys with whom I had lived and worked at Headquarters' Company, 2nd Brigade, 101st Airborne Division, Airmobile since April, 1970. Celebrating my survival and expectation that I would soon get the hell out of there came in the form of grilling of a huge steak that a buddy pilfered from the mess hall for just the occasion. I sure appreciated it, and those of us present enjoyed a delicious outdoor meal together.

Inconceivably, right after that, I made a foolish and almost catastrophic mistake that could have prevented me from starting my trip back to the States the next day. A friend, who happened to have access to a company Jeep, and I decided to drive off of base to buy an item from the local villagers, an item that to this day I cannot remember what it was. It could have been booze, it could have been marijuana or hashish, or it could have been an even more frivolous thing like a six-pack of Coca

Our company's captain and first sergeant seemed to ignore two buddies who were clowning around.

Cola, a bag of potato chips, or even some pretzels. I honestly cannot recall what seemed to be so important for the two of us to have at that time of night.

And no, in case you wondered, it wasn't a ride to find female companionship, either. With just a short time before my United Airlines flight back to the States from Da Nang, I did not feel in an amorous mood at all. I just wanted to survive my incredibly short status in Phu Bai until I could experience the wonderful feeling of my plane lifting off the tarmac.

Well, when the driver, Richard, and I, carrying an M-16 rifle, arrived at our destination outside the perimeter of the camp a few minutes later, twenty-five or thirty children of all ages from the nearby village suddenly surrounded us. Lots of them all at once—they swarmed around us with mischievous intent. Our Jeep had no roof and carried a standard array of military items, and in seconds there were lots of little hands grabbing everything not bolted or tied down.

My buddy and I got out of the Jeep, another big mistake. We attempted to control the mayhem but only accomplished giving the mob of kids an opportunity to get even

Armed with an M-16, I stood atop a bunker outside the base at Phu Bai.

closer to us. I felt helpless because the youngsters had us surrounded and the Jeep blocked. I certainly couldn't fire my M-16 at children, regardless of how out-of-control they became—the go-to means of protection served no purpose in that situation.

Furthermore, we couldn't just drive away from the wild scene around us because we could go nowhere without our vehicle hitting some of those kids. As Richard and I stood in disbelief outside the Jeep, I realized the children could easily reach into my back pocket and steal my wallet, filled with all my identification, money, and recent military orders pertaining to my departure. I quickly reached back and held it as close to my body as I could.

Within seconds, a dozen different little hands grabbed for that wallet, and one of them succeeded. I just couldn't handle the many children all around me at one time. My heart sank as I felt my wallet snatched from my hand.

Immediately the mob of children yelled triumphantly and scampered off into the darkness towards their village. I could not believe what had just happened and felt sick to my stomach.

Richard and I couldn't do anything except return to our base camp. I had no identification, no money, and no official orders confirming my scheduled departure the next day. I also had lost a list painstakingly compiled over the past couple of weeks of names, home addresses, and phone numbers of everyone I had associated with in my unit. I felt nauseated by losing that list not only for obvious security concerns but also because I counted on it to enable me to stay in touch with Army friends once we all had returned to the States.

The whole nightly affair turned into a complete disaster made worse because it was totally unnecessary. Here now for a second time I foolishly ignored that I was in an active war zone with all the accompanying risks to life and limb. Instead, I had treated the hours before my imminent departure as some sort of opportunity for an adventurous lark off the base. Without any ID or paper orders, I didn't know if my superiors would allow me to leave the next day.

I went to my hooch where I agonized as the night slipped away, and I then waited for the coming sunrise with a feeling of real dread.

Suddenly I heard my name called over our company's loudspeaker. The voice ordered me to report to a building on the base. I had no idea what to expect when I arrived at that unfamiliar building in the early morning hours. I feared I could be in serious trouble over what had happened, so I in no way anticipated the happiness and overwhelming relief I felt when a security officer met me and informed me a member of my division had returned my wallet a short time earlier. Officials had been working since then to locate me and get in touch.

My money, of course, was gone, and my list of names and home addresses had disappeared as well. But my identification card and official orders were still there, and I rejoiced. I could not believe my good fortune. Within hours of the theft of my wallet with all of my personal records and papers, somehow it had been found and returned with my ID and departure orders intact. What were the chances of that, especially the same night?

Even years later, the only possible explanation I can come up with is that when the rampaging youngsters returned to their village that night and the theft became apparent to the elders, they did not want to have any unnecessary trouble with their allies in the 101st Airborne Division just down the road. I figure if that's what happened, one of the elders returned my wallet and what they found of its contents as soon as they could that very same night.

Regardless of what actually happened to my wallet, it obviously was a pretty miraculous ending to that traumatic night and allowed me to board the C-130 transport plane a few hours later for my flight to Da Nang and eventual return to the States.

After landing at Da Nang Air Base, superiors ordered me to stay close to the area where I would soon board a United Airlines plane. Of course, I had no trouble following those orders, because there was no way that I wanted to miss that plane. After a brief stopover in Japan for refueling, that airplane would take me to a military base in California where I would receive my honorable discharge orders from the US Army.

The discharge entailed a long process that predictably involved endless lines, examinations, and paperwork. But I felt so pumped up and hyper that I handled all of the hassle in stride. I was especially happy because, back in Vietnam a few months earlier, I had made the risky decision to stay in country an additional two months.

Had I completely gone off the deep end, you ask? Well, maybe so, but I had what was to me a good reason for that decision. I decided to do it based on the new military policy of the Nixon administration that allowed a soldier like me who had been stationed overseas to be eligible for complete discharge from the US Army if he or she landed back in the States with less than 150 days left in his service commitment of twenty-four months. Otherwise, if I had done the standard tour of duty overseas of twelve months' duration, I would have had to do an additional six months of active military service at a base somewhere in the States before I had fulfilled my twenty-four-month commitment. I learned President Nixon adopted the new policy as part of his overall war plan to reduce the number of US troops serving in South Vietnam.

I thought I could safely complete the extra two months in South Vietnam for a number of reasons. I felt relatively secure on that base camp in Phu Bai where I lived and worked. Even though my eventual discharge designated me a combat veteran, I never fired my M-16 in actual combat there. My ongoing concern about reassignment to an infantry unit out in the field diminished considerably because of the small number of additional days I would be required to serve. Furthermore, I more or less enjoyed the more relaxed atmosphere within my headquarters' office due to the arrival of the new first sergeant as well as the extra privileges that accompanied my promotion to the rank of sergeant.

Of course, I did take a risk to stay two more months in a designated war zone regardless of what position I held over there, but by then I wanted so badly to be out of the military that I chose the extra two-months-and-out option. Would I make that same choice again if I found myself in the same situation? I honestly don't know, but fortunately it worked out well for me back in 1971.

I received my military discharge papers at the base in California along with the distinct honor of being awarded several service medals including a Bronze Star Medal inscribed with my name, a similarly inscribed US Army Commendation Medal, and a South Vietnamese Service Medal with Valor. Immediately, I called my parents to let them know I had made it safely back in the States. Needless to say, that was a happy call.

Then I joined two other just discharged soldiers in celebrating our new freedom by ordering and devouring delicious steak after delicious steak in a nearby restaurant. What a great sense of freedom we all felt. We then checked into the nearest motel we could find and crashed for the next forty-eight hours or so.

After that, I continued to feel absolutely euphoric. Honestly, I don't think I slept at all for the next three or four days, but the missed sleep didn't slow me down at all. I had left that war in South Vietnam, successfully completed my military obligation, and could freely live my life as I chose.

My wife, Silvia, and I visited an old Spanish fort in Pampatar, Margarita, during our stay in Venezuela in the early 1980s.

Silvia and I Make a Life in Venezuela

Okay. Please allow me to fast forward the next ten years when I

- got married and divorced
- sought and underwent psychological counseling
- worked as a teaching tennis professional at four clubs and facilities in the greater Boston area
- went to graduate school for two years and received a master's degree in social work from Boston University
- drove a yellow taxi nights in Cambridge, Massachusetts, to pay the bills while going to graduate school and for a time after graduation and
- then worked for that state's Department of Family and Children in the Child Abuse, Child Neglect Unit in Boston, two public in-patient psychiatric hospitals in the area, and
- last, for the Department of Mental Health on a crisis-intervention team called "MORT" (Mobile Outreach Team) just north of Boston

Looking back on that span of ten years, I don't know how the hell I handled all of it. It exhausts me physically and emotionally just thinking about that incredibly turbulent time of my life. Of course, being drafted into the Army just months after graduating from Tufts University was a major change in the direction of my life back then, but I felt like the change was forced upon me. When I got out of the Army about a year and a half later, the circumstances were quite different in that the direction that my life would take was entirely up to me, and for the next several years, I struggled mightily with that issue.

It really wasn't until little Stephanie was born in 1987 that my focus shifted to providing for my family. Before that huge event in our lives, I think Silvia and I kind of drifted through life together. Once Stephanie came into our lives, our attention focused on being the best parents we could be for the sake of our child.

But somehow I did survive that ten years, and one day in 1980 during the time I worked in downtown Boston for the state Department of Family and Children, I agreed to help my secretary move on the following weekend.

Little did I know that a minor decision like that would end up momentous. When the weekend arrived and I helped move my friend's stuff from one apartment to another, she introduced me to a Venezuelan friend of hers named Silvia Cecilia Abreu. Silvia was studying for a degree in mass communication at Emerson College in Boston, while her brother, Hernan, had enrolled for a degree in chemical engineering at nearby Northeastern University. Even though Silvia was a native of Caracas, Venezuela, and spoke little English, it didn't take long for us to be a couple after that first introduction.

After the failure of my first brief marriage, I lived in a tiny room of a building that offered weekly rentals in Boston's Kenmore Square. It was an easy walk for me to visit with Silvia in her apartment on Hemenway Street in the Fenway area. She shared her place with her cousin and another young woman from Venezuela. Her brother had an apartment one floor below.

After I got out of work and Silvia completed the day's studies, we often got together and went to a local eatery for a slice of pizza or maybe a delicious sub. On weekends we enjoyed spending time at the reserved garden plot I had cultivated just a short walk away in the adjacent Boston Victory Gardens. We enjoyed harvesting fresh green beans, tomatoes, peas, blackberries, lettuce, and carrots from that little garden. The blackberries came as a special treat to us because their bushes already grew in the plot assigned me by the Victory Garden committee. Along with the blackberry bushes, the former tenant had left an empty wooden tool box big enough for us to use as a wooden bench with a top.

I remember one time I used that bench as a place to stretch out while enjoying the sun's rays. Unbeknownst to me, Silvia had come from her apartment to the garden plot to spend some time with me after I told her earlier I'd be there. Well, when Silvia approached the plot, she didn't see me because I was laid out on the bench against the bushes. She was about to get suspicious, thinking perhaps she had caught me fibbing about my whereabouts when, all of a sudden, I popped up from the bench. I told her she didn't need to worry about where I was because I was right where I said I would be all along. We've shared a good laugh about that one more than once over the years.

Other weekends, we would jump into my car and, with no particular destination in mind, drive into rural areas of northern New England for the day to explore the many intriguing dirt roads to see where they led. Oftentimes those isolated roads would lead us to an interesting general store, a small hamlet, or an area of unexpected scenic beauty. I remember a trip when we drove up to one of those northern states during the foliage season, and I stopped to take pictures of Silvia silhouetted against spectacular leaf colors of red, orange, and yellow.

When she was a young woman in Venezuela, Silvia had dreamed of becoming a professional photographer, and even though that did not come to reality, she has always appreciated scenes that would interest a photographer.

Another time, Silvia and I drove to a coastal town in central Maine for an overnight trip. I loved the idea of introducing her to the world of camping, an outdoor activity that I had always enjoyed. I drove a pickup truck at the time, and by the time we arrived at the secluded beach on the ocean I thought would be a terrific spot for us to camp, it wasn't long before we both struggled to adjust to the cold temperatures that met us as we began setting up our tent on the smooth sand.

Silvia was a good sport about it, and we shared a good laugh about the frigid conditions on that windswept beach until a short time later I realized poor Silvia was almost a solid block of ice. Naturally, being from Venezuela, she was not used to the strong, cold winds of Maine. It also meant her first experience at sleeping in a sleeping bag in a two-person tent.

As we tried to stay warm in that flimsy tent, nature called, and I decided (instead of going out in that freezing cold) I would unzip the door flap and relieve myself while leaning out of the opening. Midway through that escapade, I got a horrendous cramp in my leg and found myself in an unbelievably awkward and painful position. The exposed half of me was freezing while the other half was in pain from the cramp. And all of that while I desperately tried to relieve myself. As much of a disaster as it was for me, Silvia found the whole scene hilariously funny. Later, I had to agree with her.

We retreated to our truck in the parking lot and spent what can only be described as a memorable night huddled together in the vehicle's cab. I don't remember that I suggested to her the possibility of us going camping together again for quite a while after that adventure.

Although I was gun-shy about marriage after my painful divorce just a few years earlier and I consequently ran from my relationship with Silvia more than once during our courtship, she had incredible patience with me.

After a brief breakup, when we got together again and I proposed to her, she didn't want to be patient any longer. She asked that we be married in two weeks. When I shook off the shock, I agreed to do just that. We quickly called friends and family to let them know and to see if they would be available to attend the ceremony on such short notice. Incredibly, everyone, including my parents from Connecticut and Silvia's parents from Venezuela, made time to attend our civil wedding ceremony, presided over by a justice of the peace.

We got married in the apartment of a Venezuelan friend in Brookline, Massachusetts, in August, 1980 and then lived together in the Hemenway Street apartment for the next several months.

Despite not yet having a command of English, Silvia did very well in her courses at Emerson College. I admired her for that. Good grief, college courses are often hard enough without having to complete them in a language you don't know well. And she and I were able to converse in English with each other from Day One in our relationship, even though it was a little tough in the beginning. Her mastery of English seemed to improve daily.

I believe Silvia's mass-communication skills came naturally because she came from a home where almost every day famous musical and entertainment figures surrounded her and her younger brother. Her father, a famous musician, composer, and conductor, often entertained fellow artists, some of them celebrities, in their home. Silvia's mom worked at the public university, and that influence may have rubbed off, too.

Silvia often attended concerts and musical competitions where her well-known and respected father served as maestro for the evening. Silvia no doubt enjoyed being under the bright lights with her father, and he tremendously liked sharing those exciting moments with her. I am sure that her early personal experiences helped her

My father-in-law, Anibal Abreu, conducts his orchestra in the 1970s.

to navigate through the many challenges of obtaining her undergraduate degree in a foreign country.

However, after Silvia graduated with a bachelor's degree in mass communication in 1981, the two of us faced a big decision. She had attended Emerson on a Venezuelan government scholarship grant that obligated her to return to her country for employment there in her field of expertise for at least two years. I had a job with the state Department of Mental Health. Incredibly, Silvia and I hadn't previously discussed the big issue that now stood before us: Does Silvia return to her native country for those two years while I continue my work on the outreach team in Massachusetts? Or do I leave my current job and join Silvia in Caracas for those two years?

What would be the state of our marriage if we lived separately for two years? If I went with Silvia to her South American country, how would I handle communication? I barely spoke or understood Spanish. Where would I work? Obviously, these major issues posed a quandary for the two of us. We were on a short leash when it came to time for making a decision. In the end, I decided to resign from my job and go to Venezuela with Silvia. I trusted that I could manage to learn enough Spanish to allow me to live and work in Caracas and that I could also find employment there that would provide me a source of income for the next two years. I sold the meager amount of furniture I had accumulated up to then. I made sure I had a current, valid US passport and bade farewell to Boston area friends.

Now, I'll share with you what transpired over the following approximately twenty-four months in the singular country of Venezuela. As our airplane approached the airport in Venezuela, from one side of the plane I could see the magnificent expanse of the Caribbean Sea. From the other side, I could see part of a mountain populated by ranchos, homes of low-income and impoverished people. At night, the spectacular view causes some Venezuelans to say, "With all of the lights on, it looks like a Nativity scene." My first impression of the country struck me with awe.

Passengers awarded the pilot a loud and happy round of applause for a good flight and smooth landing on that July day in 1981. My wife and I disembarked at Simon Bolivar International Airport, the area's main airport, in Maiquetia in the Vargas state separated from Caracas by a long chain of mountains. Silvia mentioned that Caracas nestled in a long valley on the other side of the mountains.

After a a seemingly endless process of immigration and claiming baggage, Silvia's parents, Anibal and Gisela Abreu, greeted us warmly in Arrivals. After a forty-five minute drive, they welcomed us into their home, a modern apartment in a high-rise near downtown Caracas. We would live there with them throughout our stay.

Soon after Silvia and I moved into her parents' apartment, I attended, as guest of honor, the wedding anniversary of Julio, one of Silvia's uncles. There I met Silvia's wonderful family, including her grandmother, uncles, aunts, and cousins of every look and age. A precious and united family with no generational gaps, they welcomed me warmly in Spanish as if we had always known each other. Thank goodness some who spoke English rescued me as I tried to converse.

The seventh child of a family of ten including six girls and four boys, Julio was Gisela's brother. A smart, beautiful, and strong woman who had decided in her youth to stop pursuing her bachelor's degree at a technical school, Gisela worked to help support her large birth family. Later, she married Anibal. After bringing up their two children, she decided to go back to work and was employed until her retirement as administrative assistant in the department of biology at Central University of Venezuela.

*My father-in-law, Anibal Abreu, plays piano with a group of Venezuelan musicians. above,
early in his career, top, previous page, and at Radio Caracas TV, bottom, previous page.
He displays one of his many awards, right.*

Gisela unexpectedly died in 2000 in her early seventies from a blood clot in her leg, possibly started by a bite from a Brown Recluse spider. The painful loss affected all of us. I admired her and truly adored her as my mother-in-law. Despite our difficulty in communicating in each other's native language, she and I understood and respected each other. I loved her and miss her.

Silvia's father, Anibal Abreu, the son of a Venezuelan native named Carmen Rosa, endured a difficult childhood because of his father's early passing but persevered and enjoyed a career as a successful musician his entire adult life. He started by playing piano for a local radio station when he was seventeen. Despite not having received formal music training, his natural talent propelled him to become a well-known composer, arranger, and orchestra conductor as well as musical director for two major Venezuelan TV stations, first at Radio Caracas TV and then for twenty-six years at Venevision. He also won prestigious awards in international music festivals. Silvia and I attended one.

Anibal's other musical accomplishments include being arranger for the island of Aruba's national anthem when Aruba gained independence. He was among founders of the Association of Writers and Composers of Venezuela. His sense of humor shines forth when he reverses a common saying to state: "I was a musician because I couldn't be a doctor." At eighty-eight, to his credit, he remains active in the Venezuelan music scene.

A family story begins with Anibal playing piano at Radio Caracas when he was seventeen. He accompanied Ernesto Garcia singing for radio listeners. The two young men also pitched for competing baseball teams, but they didn't realize it until they became good friends in the months ahead. Ernesto met his future wife, Elbia, at a party they attended, and it wasn't long before Anibal began dating her sister, Gisela. She eventually married Anibal and gave birth to a daughter, Silvia, and son, Hernan. Ernesto, now ninety, and I still enjoy a strong friendship.

Ernesto and Elbia Garcia, our beloved friends, often hung out with my wife, Silvia, and me when we were in Caracas.

My wife, Silvia, pauses at her job producing educational TV programs in Caracas in the early 1980s.

Once Silvia and I got ourselves settled in her parents' apartment, it was time for us to find gainful employment. After a bit of a search, she landed a good job in the government's department of education, where she produced noteworthy educational programing for public television.

As far as my job prospects were concerned, before we had even left the United States, Silvia learned that a modern and popular coastal resort called the Macuto-Sheraton Hotel, about an hour's drive from Caracas, had advertised to hire its first tennis professional. Whoever the hotel hired would provide tennis lessons for its guests, hold occasional tournaments, and manage its court facilities. Despite not having taught nor even played tennis for several years since I obtained my master's degree, I contacted the Sheraton about the position. I received a letter from the hotel manager advising me to go there for a job interview as soon as I got to Venezuela and obtained necessary work authorizations. *Have Racquet, Will Travel* reappeared in my life in a very adventurous and memorable way.

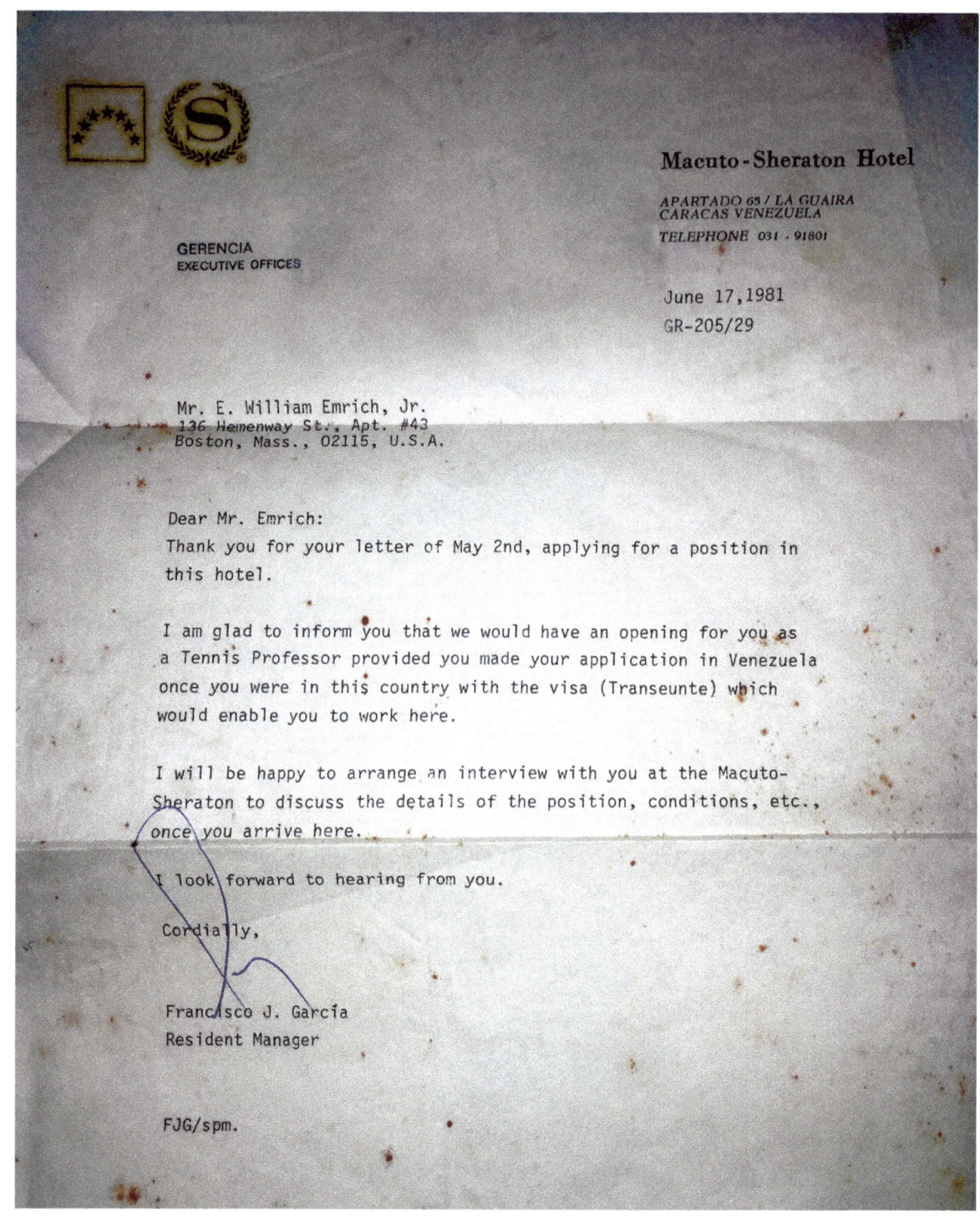

In June, 1981, before Silvia and I moved to Venezuela, I received a letter from the Macuto-Sheraton manager informing me of an opening for Tennis Professional at the hotel.

My wife drove me to the resort hotel a couple of days later to meet with the Sheraton executive in charge of hiring. Fortunately for me, he spoke English very well, and soon he offered me the position of Tennis Professional. However, and this

From the tennis courts, pros and players had a view of the hotel.

was the kicker for me, I got the job offer on condition that I immediately prove to him that I could play tennis. He called into his office the manager of the resort hotel, Señor Francisco Garcia, introduced us, and asked Señor Garcia to change into his athletic clothes and play a game of tennis with me.

Whoa. I certainly hadn't anticipated that I would have to prove I could play tennis during my job interview. I mean, I had been playing tennis since I was four years old. My father used to hit balls to me when on the tennis courts at the Shore & Country Club, where we belonged and where my parents met many years before. I loved every minute of it. I've told you about my later employment with Walter Debany, the head pro at Shore & Country. As his assistant pro, I began my money-making tennis career.

Before and during my time with Walter and at the encouragement of both my mother and father, I played tennis every summer at the club, then played in New England tournaments during my teens. I earned an official ranking of #4 in the Age 13 and Under category in all of New England and had a place on the region's prestigious Wright Cup Team. Later, I played on both my high school and college tennis teams. I also worked as tennis pro for four tennis facilities in Massachusetts after returning from Vietnam, including the renowned Hazel Hotchkiss Wightman Tennis Center in Weston (where I also taught squash), the Nashawtuc Country Club in Concord, the Heritage Pool and Racquet Club, also in Concord, and the Reservoir Racquet Club in Framingham.

I had never before been told I needed to show I could play the game as a condition of hiring. And not only would I have to prove that I could play, but I had to do it against my future boss, the manager of the resort.

Of course, Señor Garcia agreed to the proposal. He had to. His superior asked him to do it, so he couldn't say no. He quickly found some tennis clothes that fit me as well as a tennis racquet I could use, and off we went to the tennis court area of the resort. That consisted of two hard-surfaced courts surrounded by a high metal fence. They looked out over the lovely expanses of the Caribbean Sea.

Now I knew I was in a bind. I hoped against hope I could come out of the situation with my tennis credentials and new job offer intact. To label me rusty after literally years of not playing tennis would constitute a big understatement. Plus, and I mean a gigantic, worrisome plus, when I last played those many years ago, I had no backhand stroke. For some reason, back in 1975 and 1976, during the last couple of years when I taught and played tennis in the States, I developed a huge mental block (I think referred to in the golfing community as "suffering from the yips") whenever my opponent hit a tennis ball to my left side and I needed to respond with a backhand shot. Consequently, I either stubbornly tried to hit the backhand and ended up making an embarrassingly bad shot or I compensated by running to my left and then attempting to hit the ball with a forehand shot. Neither proved a good solution to the problem, especially since I had a previous record as a very good tennis player at both forehand and backhand and, thus, expected to have a sound game as a professional teacher.

When I changed to an entirely different line of work, namely psychiatric social work, the decision inadvertently rescued me from myself and the yip when I had to hit a backhand. The mental block didn't cause me to switch careers, but it definitely created an issue I would have had to address if I continued as a working tennis pro.

Little did I know it would rear its ugly head years later while I searched for employment in South America.

Another problem I characterized as more political. If I played well and beat my future boss—and unfortunately I could tell from the moment he stepped onto the court with me that he was a very competitive man—how would he react to losing? Would I be on his s--t list from Day One on the job? Or, if I played badly and Señor Garcia won, would the hiring executive rescind the job offer?

What to do? What to do?

Well, frankly, I didn't have a whole lot of time to figure out the best position to take in that awkward and uncomfortable situation. I quickly opted for the play-your-best-tennis-and-consequences-be-damned approach. The hotel manager showed himself a pretty good player, but the tennis gods definitely smiled on me that day. Despite playing around my missing backhand the entire time, I ended up winning every game that we played to finish at 6-0, 6-0. And, at least on the surface, Señor Garcia was gracious in defeat. He appeared to take the whole experience in stride.

After the two of us had washed up a little bit and returned to the executive's office, I found myself signing my name to an employment contract. Handshakes went all around as I agreed to be the first and only tennis professional of the Macuto-Sheraton Hotel and Resort in Venezuela.

With a job and source of income for the foreseeable future, I had to figure out how the heck I would teach tennis and run the South American resort's tennis program without knowing how to speak Spanish. That issue had come up only briefly during my job interview when the hiring executive encouraged me to become more proficient in the language. Surprisingly, the issue didn't appear to be a big deal. Maybe the chief executive felt most of the guests at his hotel would know some English or he was confident I would soon learn his native language adequately to satisfy the demands of the job.

Since I had to report to work at the resort in just a few days, I had to come up with a quick temporary solution to this challenging problem. I also had to try dutifully to learn more and more Spanish each day during the next several months. The temporary solution involved, thankfully, the willingness of my wife to teach me a few essential phrases that I would use in my tennis lessons at the resort, such as "Bend your knees," "Keep your eyes focused on the ball," and "Turn sideways to the net when you are hitting the ball." I memorized several such phrases and headed off to my first working day at the Macuto-Sheraton.

In order to qualify for the job as Profesor de Tenis, I had to demonstrate my ability to play versus the resident manager, Francisco Garcia, right.

Fortunately, my first day as El Profesor de Tenis went reasonably well. I met the two or three hotel employees who would work with me to schedule tennis lessons, reserve courts, and help keep all things regarding tennis running smoothly. However, I realized immediately that this workplace would be one that I had not experienced before. I didn't have a bad feeling or feel disappointed, but I felt as if I had been dropped into the challenging situation in a sink-or-swim way.

A perceived lack of support or even interest from higher-ups in the resort hotel bothered me. For example, I soon realized that, aside from catching a glimpse of my manager walking through my general area in the early morning hours as part of his daily rounds, I would have no other contact with him for the rest of the day. At this moment, you may be thinking that lack of contact with the boss wasn't necessarily a bad thing. Perhaps it meant that he felt confident about my ability to do the job. However, for me, it said that nobody in management really cared about what happened way over there in the tennis area as long the hotel guests did not complain.

I realized that, as long as I showed up on the job for at least part of each day and nothing worthy of concern happened around the tennis courts, I could expect a check at the end of the month. I tried to make do with what I had there, but it wasn't much. I had a tiny bungalow facing the tennis courts for storage of gear and supplies. It was a far cry from the attractive tennis shops that I was used to in the States that offered the latest in tennis clothes and tennis equipment. The tiny storage room barely had a lock on the door and very little to prevent anyone from breaking in if so inclined. I confirmed my observation months later when I caught a fellow hotel employee casually stealing a pair of my tennis sneakers out of my supposedly secure unit.

And a couple of weeks after I had started the job, I learned I would not even be allowed to choose and purchase the tennis attire I wanted. One day, out of the blue, management asked me to accompany a hotel employee into Caracas, a good hour's drive away from the hotel. The destination? A sporting store where the hotel employee and store clerk chose tennis shorts and shirts for me without input from me, the person who would wear the outfits. I really disliked how I felt and looked in those newly purchased clothes. I only wore them at the hotel for a few days until I thought I could safely go back to shorts and shirts much more to my liking.

I found the whole experience a little odd and strangely impersonal. I probably needed to remind myself that I worked not in the United States but in Venezuela, a South American country with a very different culture. Also, I needed to remind myself that possibly I represented something new and different to my Venezuelan co-workers. I am sure they wanted to "check this new gringo out" and see what kind of person they were dealing with before they trusted me. They also probably didn't know what to expect from the first tennis pro at the resort hotel, especially since I hailed from a different country and didn't speak their language. Thankfully, over time, I sensed they felt more and more comfortable both working and socializing with me—and I with them.

One woman I got to know pretty well through the tennis program merits a special mention in this narrative. Young, pleasant, poised, and easy to engage in conversation, Maria had a crooked jaw. Because we had become friends, one day I asked her about it. Much to my horror, I learned that she had been born and raised in Argentina and was a teenager during that country's military government brutal crackdown on opposition to its heavy-handed leadership. The government's opposition to anyone perceived as socialist or leftist included an attempt to eliminate guerrilla forces active in mountainous regions of the country. Military officers tortured and killed friends and family members suspected of aiding those rebels.

Unfortunately for Maria, her brother joined rebel forces bivouacked somewhere in the hills. When government henchmen discovered the fact, they paid a visit to that young man's family. My friend's jaw was broken during the brutal interrogation that followed, but she told me she did not give up the whereabouts of her brother even in the doubtful case that she knew. Her severely crooked jaw from her nightmarish treatment by government soldiers in Argentina stayed with her in a public way even as she lived in Venezuela. I admired her when I knew her back then and frankly will always admire her for her bravery and inner strength. Knowing what she went through has a way of keeping things in proper perspective in our own lives, don't you think?

Over the next few weeks, I got into a pretty good routine at my job, mixing in teaching tennis lessons to players of all ages, getting to know the regulars who showed up at the tennis courts each week, and gaining insight into how a typical day as the tennis professional there would proceed.

It certainly wasn't a stressful job. The more stressful part of my routine actually involved the long drive to and from the hotel that I made six days a week in my wife's little car. The Macuto-Sheraton was in a section of the coast called La Caraballeda. To its east, several popular beaches ending in the area of Los Caracas claimed the coastline. To the hotel's west lay the coastal area called El Litoral Central.

When I headed back to the apartment in Caracas, what started out as a busy, local thoroughfare from the hotel through El Litoral Central soon turned into a major highway that took you past the big airport in Maiquetia where most of the country's international air travel took place. Once you passed the airport, soon you had to drive through a series of tunnels blasted through a series of mountains years before to allow residents of Caracas access to the fabulous coastal area.

I thought drivers in Boston behaved terribly and sometimes genuinely obnoxiously, but those people were minor leaguers compared to Venezuelan drivers. Drivers of Caracas thought nothing of blaring their car horns whenever they wanted, cutting your vehicle off without a moment's notice, and driving at a speed only race car drivers should be allowed to achieve.

From the tennis courts, we had a view of the public beach and coastline

And there was an added pleasure (or not) of driving in Venezuela's capital city and its suburbs. The huge metropolitan area of Caracas rested in a wide, deep valley surrounded by imposing mountains. On the mountainsides were thousands of small, rickety homes, mostly shacks really, housing extremely poor residents of the city. Many of those makeshift homes, called ranchos in Spanish, ended up dangerously vulnerable not only to criminals who lived among them, but also to horrific mudslides whenever heavy rains pummeled the area. Apparently the residents felt

A woman sold empanadas at Camuri Chico Beach on El Litoral, top, previous page. Silvia, her Cousin Lizbeth, and her Canadian friend, Kevin, enjoyed the beach in El Litoral, bottom, previous page. Devotees placed a Nativity scene on the sands at La Guaira, Venezuela, in the early 1980s, top. Life preservers, buoys, and rubber rafts piled up outside a storefront in the Litoral, above.

they had nowhere else to go, because they often rebuilt their fragile homes in the same precarious locations year after year.

The additional pleasure (am I allowed to be sarcastic here?) that I refer to is that young and desperate rancho inhabitants viewed the many car drivers passing through their area of the highway as potential sources of free money, jewelry, and assorted valuables. Every driver on that highway to and from Caracas had the very real possibility of being robbed at gunpoint by lawless Venezuelan men patrolling their part of the highway on motorbikes or motorcycles in search of the next victim. When they decided upon a specific driver, usually because that person was stuck in bumper to bumper traffic or stopped at a traffic light, they drove up to the side of the vehicle, flashed their weapons, and demanded that all the people in the car hand over their wallets, purses, and jewelry. Such a frightening event happens within seconds. Then the gunmen more often than not successfully escaped because, unlike their victims, they could quickly weave through traffic on motorbikes or motorcycles until they disappear.

A lesser version of this horrible experience occurred when innocent drivers or passengers in moving vehicles suddenly felt their watches snatched from their wrists

Ranchos, or homes for the very poor, strung out along the litoral.

by someone riding next to them on the highway on a motorcycle or motorbike. When motivated by a little more daring or desperation, the perpetrator would reach into a vehicle's open window and grab whatever valuable was available to them, say, a woman's purse lying on the seat. Sometimes they would even deftly break and snatch away a gold chain hanging from the neck of a driver or passenger.

To emphasize how unsafe were the streets or highways of Caracas and its suburbs, I will relate to you the harrowing experience one of my wife's cousins suffered years later when she drove on the city's dangerous streets. Two men suddenly entered the car she drove, threw her into the backseat, tied her up, and drove around the city while discussing out loud what they should do with the horrified young woman at their mercy in the backseat. She remembers hearing one of the two men saying that they should kill her. Thank God they ended up not physically harming her. Eventually, by some miracle, they let her go free, but of course the episode absolutely terrified her.

As for police professionalism and protection (or lack of it) on those same Venezuelan streets and highways, consider a comical but real example of what you should expect if you happened to be the victim of a crime, or in this case, simply involved in a minor car accident.

Several years ago, one of my relatives from the States visited Venezuela. She and some of her friends from the Caracas area got into a fender bender. They pulled their car over to the side of the road and waited for police to arrive and hopefully get the necessary paperwork completed rapidly so they could continue on their way. An hour went by, and so did several police cars. Not one police car stopped to help.

Two, then three hours went by as did many more police cars before finally a law enforcement officer stopped his vehicle at the scene. During that horrendously long time waiting for a policeman to show up, my relative became so hot and restless that she popped open a bottle of beer stored in the car. She worried that the officer would see the open bottle, so she hid it along the roadside. But apparently she really had no need to worry about that issue, because her Venezuelan friends with her assured her that it would not be a big deal to any policeman.

Sure enough, when the officer stopped his police cruiser and walked over to them, my relative's friends offered a beer to the guy. He accepted. All present had a little beer party on the side of the highway while the law enforcement official investigated the car accident. Can you imagine that happening on the roadways of the United States?? I didn't think so.

My tales emphasize how going to and from my tennis job at the Macuto-Sheraton made for major adventure every day. I recall one late afternoon drive home when a public bus bumped into my car just a few minutes after I left the hotel on my way back to Caracas. It just so happened that day that I had a Venezuelan passenger in the car with me, a female employee at the Sheraton, because her own car had broken down and she needed a ride back to her residence. Well, when the big commercial bus nicked my car, my passenger insisted I chase down the bus so she could give the bus driver a few choice words. I ended up chasing that damned bus for several blocks through the city streets but never could get close enough to it to allow my passenger to let loose with her verbal volleys. I felt like I was in the middle of an action movie as I swerved around cars and tried to outrun the bus driver, all to the sounds of the screaming and yelling of enthusiastic words of encouragement my passenger freely offered. It turned out to be a hilarious ride, but please don't tell my wife, because it was her car that I drove so recklessly.

We drove a blue Renault when we lived in Venezuela in the early 1980s.

One interesting occurrence at work in those first three or four weeks involved the food that I ate at the hotel. Now, it is no secret that I love to eat. My wife, family members, and friends will readily attest to that. And I pretty much will eat anything set before me, with very few exceptions. But the first time I ate lunch as a hotel employee tested my passion for consuming a good meal. I understood that my job included lunch, and I should eat with the other employees. That sounded fine with me.

When a co-worker ushered me into an employee-only area of the main building for the first time, I quickly realized that once again I had stepped into an unfamiliar world. From fifteen to twenty fellow employees, every one of them I surmised of Venezuelan nationality, gathered in the depressing-looking room around a huge cooking pot set on the floor. They held out bowls provided by the hotel.

One of the crew from the hotel kitchen dished out an appropriate serving of what I found out later Spanish speakers call mondongo, a Venezuelan specialty. I dug in after the cook filled up my bowl and immediately added a new item to my very short mental list of foods never to be eaten by me again. Mondongo, I learned later, is made not only from pigs' feet and vegetables, but also from cows' intestines. I can pretty much guarantee that if you haven't been brought up eating the stuff, upon trying it, that you, like me, will permanently cross it off your own list of acceptable meals.

Of course, everyone else in that Venezuelan-dominated room enjoyed the heck out of the facility's lunch offering that day, and that was absolutely fine. Since that was the only choice, my stomach would go empty for several long hours until I could return to the apartment in Caracas and enjoy the delicious soups, salads, and assorted other wonderful meals that Gisela, my wonderful mother-in-law, regularly prepared.

And here enters Mr. Ronald Tacon.

Born and raised in the United States, Ron went to college to study hotel management. He did well, and upon receiving his bachelor's degree, he landed a trainee position with the Sheraton chain. Not long after, he received his first trainee assignment to the Macuto-Sheraton Hotel in Caraballeda, Venezuela. Not surprisingly, since we were the only two gringo employees at the hotel as far as I could ascertain, we quickly hit it off.

When Ron found out that I had not been offered a more upscale dining environment nor a bigger choice of foods than strictly the most basic of native Venezuelan fare, he convinced the higher-ups to allow me to eat at a cafeteria-style outside food area where the hotel guests ate.

Now, I generally love traditional Venezuelan food, with its terrific soups, offerings of fresh fruits and vegetables, and delectable meat and rice combinations. So I left the stark, poorly furnished employees-only room where we twenty hungry, tired

Ron, Teresa, and their little boy, Hector, waited outside his wife's family-owned store in December, 1982.

co-workers held out our bowls for whatever food awaited us in that gigantic cooking pot in front of us. I went to a dining setting where I stood in a line of resort guests casually choosing from among the wonderfully prepared offerings of meats, fish, fruits and vegetables there.

Presented with those two very different dining experiences, the choice was clear to me. And, did I mention that I could go back for seconds at the cafeteria setting? I really appreciated Ron's voluntary and unexpected intervention on my behalf. In fact, it turned out that he got me one of the best perks of my tennis pro job at the hotel. From then on, I looked forward to lunch time.

Shortly after Sheraton hired us, management required Ron and me to attend a new employee orientation. Everyone else in that room of perhaps fifty people appeared to be either native Venezuelan or otherwise fluent in Spanish. We realized we would eventually have to stand up and introduce themselves to the others. Naturally, Señor Garcia conducted the meeting in Spanish. My new gringo friend, Ron, and I could barely put a basic sentence together in Spanish.

As we listened to several people who helped run the meeting apparently welcoming all of us and instructing us in the details of employment at the resort, it became obvious that neither Ron nor I could understand a single thing said. The absurdity of it all plus the fact that we knew we would soon be called upon to introduce ourselves in Spanish to the other participants, including our boss, Señor Garcia, got to us.

Despite our wishes to the contrary, both Ron and I began to giggle uncontrollably. We laughed as inconspicuously and quietly as possible, but how could we escape notice in that crowd? When I somehow gained a bit of control and managed to stop giggling, my American buddy started again, which of course drove me back into further laughing fits. We continued on in this way for what seemed an eternity until Ron couldn't handle it anymore and literally left the room. Even when he returned a couple of minutes later, I knew that we could not in any way make eye contact with each other or the whole episode would begin again.

By some miracle, Ron and I kept the out-of-control giggling episode to ourselves. We even managed a little bit later to introduce ourselves adequately in Spanish. Thankfully, both of us got through the rest of that orientation meeting without further incident, but I will never forget that start to my first job in Venezuela. Thank goodness I didn't get fired right there at orientation.

Days and weeks went by. I taught tennis and ran a few tournaments for resort guests. My friendship with Gringo Ron strengthened. All of a sudden, he came by to visit with a lovely Venezuelan woman who worked at the resort. A single mother of a small boy, Teresa became enamored with Ron (and vice versa) in no time at all—a whirlwind romance. Soon, Ron confided their engagement in me, but he wanted to keep it a secret so as not to cause trouble for either of them in light of a resort rule forbidding employees to date.

Within days of that surprising news, Ron and Teresa made plans for a wedding. Ron asked me to be best man. By the time the wedding actually took place, it turned out that I shared my role with a member of the bride's family. I guess that at that point, I was technically co-best man.

Within just a few days, there I stood along with Ron, the other co-best man, Señor Bozo, and Teresa before a priest in a lovely, traditional Catholic church not too far from the hotel. We listened to the bride and groom state their vows to each other. The whole scene struck me as be a bit surreal. I mean, my life had radically changed in just a few months' time. Less than six months earlier, I was working in Massachusetts as a psychiatric social worker. Silvia, my Venezuelan wife, and I lived in a small but comfortable apartment on Boston's Hemenway Street. All of a sudden I found myself

Co-best man Señor Bozo, Ron, and I, from left, waited for the wedding to begin.

Ron and Teresa with the flower girl and Teresa's son, Hector, as ring bearer, her mother, and I stood in front of the altar after the wedding.

in the South American country of Venezuela employed as a tennis professional at a spectacular seaside Caribbean resort, taking part in a wedding ceremony as co-best man for a nice fellow gringo whom I had known for only two or three months. What a lot for my head to process.

    The church ceremony went well despite that it almost didn't come off at all. People in the wedding party arrived so late that the ceremony almost got postponed for another day. Just a short time after the scheduled end of Ron and Teresa's ceremony, another wedding was set to take place. Consequently, almost no time remained for Ron and Teresa to exchange their vows before the next wedding party took their place in the church. At the time, I thought that it was going to be a major crisis for everyone present, but once again, I neglected to realize the distinctiveness of Venezuelan customs.

In Venezuela, almost nothing started when technically scheduled. If a friend told you he would see you at four in the afternoon, look for him to arrive maybe at five but certainly by six. Similarly, if a meeting or some other business or social engagement was supposed to start in fifteen minutes and last for approximately a half hour, be assured that the activity might actually begin in about forty-five minutes and probably last an hour and a half. Not infrequently, a gathering would go on deep into the night because after the initial meeting, you would probably be expected to go out to dinner and later to a bar for some nightcaps with the others.

There is nothing inherently wrong or strange with that way of doing things. In actuality, it may be the better and more enjoyable way to do things than the abiding by rigid business and social practices often admired in the United States. I wouldn't be at all surprised if the average blood pressure levels of a native South American businessman or businesswoman are lower than the averages of his/her North American cousins. Still, for a gringo like me, the customary late-night socializing of Venezuelans did take some getting used to, and in the approximately two years that I lived in that country, I don't think I ever got fully comfortable with that part of their lifestyle.

For example, one of the hardest cultural adjustments for me involved traditional times for eating meals on holidays or other formal occasions. Breakfast might start around ten in the morning, then lunch around three, and finally dinner at ten in the evening. That dinner hour was the killer for me. By the time the traditional holiday or formal dinner finished at people's homes, the clock read midnight. And then, after that, people wanted to socialize with their friends and go out to bars, nightclubs, and restaurants into the very wee hours of the morning.

My wife and her family thought nothing of visiting a favorite place for arepas or even grilled chicken at six in the morning, and that would be on their way home from a regular weekend night out. Needless to say, after experiencing one or two of those extended party hours nights, I was completely exhausted and vowing not to join the others when the next party night arrived. Of course, eating times were more flexible during work days when people's work schedules dictated their meal times.

Please forgive me for my major digression from the earlier main topic of conversation, namely, the characteristics of my work at the Macuto-Sheraton Hotel on the lovely shores of the Caribbean Sea. It turned out that my days at that Caribbean seaside resort would soon end. After about six months as tennis professional there, as exotically attractive as that job may sound, I had no interest in continuing. I stopped going to work.

One earlier incident in particular probably played a major role in my decision to leave. It happened at the tennis courts one morning. Two airline pilots from Spain came over from the hotel and wanted to play on one of the two courts. That would normally have been fine with me, but on that day I had reserved both courts for a tournament I had earlier planned for some of the tennis regulars who came by almost daily.

Coincidentally, just a few days before, I obtained permission from my manager to reserve an unused court for myself when necessary, so I felt confident I stood on firm ground when I politely told the two pilots that the court that they wanted was not then available. Well, they became very upset and stormed away. A few minutes later, they showed up again, this time accompanied by my manager. In no uncertain terms, and in front of the two pilots, he told me to allow the men to play on the court.

Getting ready for a tennis tournament, I stood between a hotel guest from the airlines, left, and Señor DiAngelotonio,

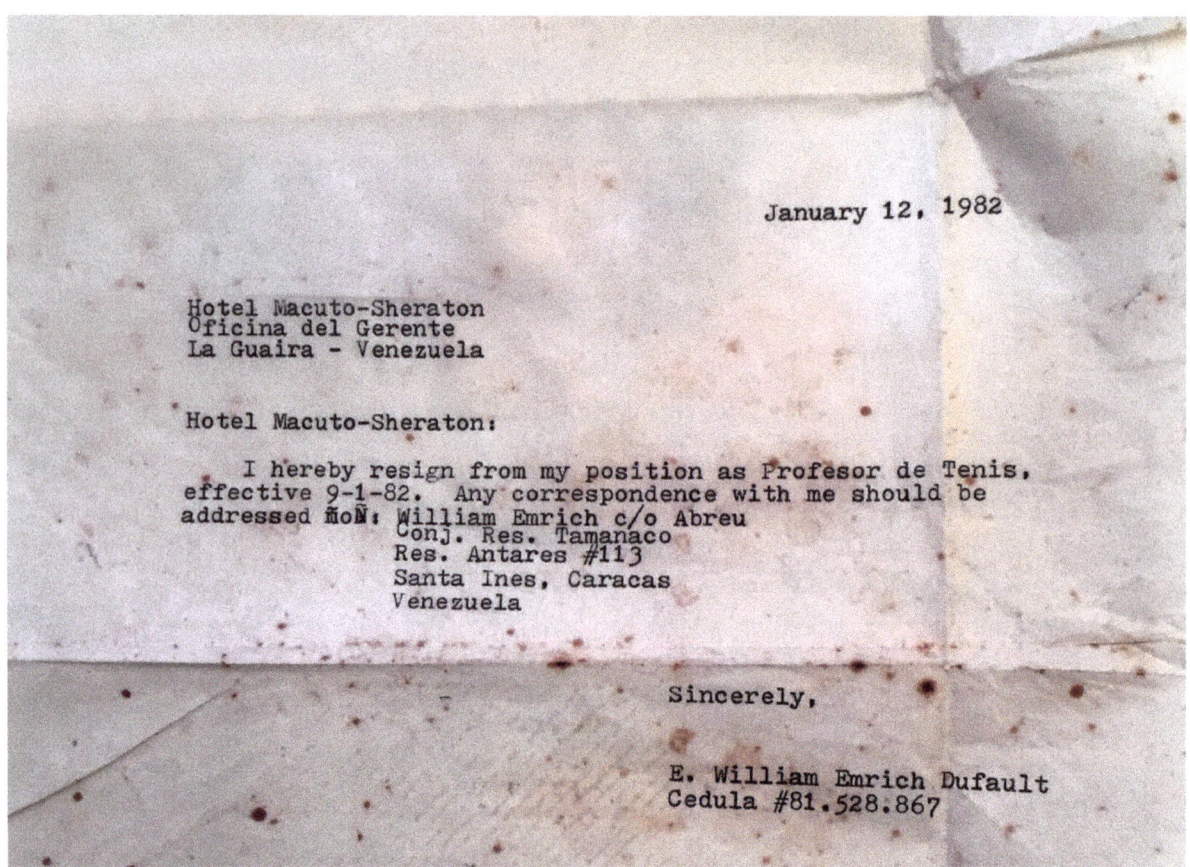

By January, 1982, after six months as Profesor de Tenis, I gave my resignation.

Needless to say, I felt humiliated and angry. Then, I became even more infuriated when the two pilots walked on the court and began arrogantly gloating over their victory and my public putdown.

When management noticed my absence after a no-show period of about a week, I received an offer to return without negative consequences, but my heart was just not in it. I returned for only an uncomfortable and awkward moment to return the tennis gear they had purchased for me months before and to retrieve the few personal items I had stored at the tennis area. My *Have Racquet, Will Travel* longtime scenario neared its end, but it managed to stay alive just a little bit longer, as you will see later.

After a two- or three-day stay with my wife at a hotel on the intriguing Venezuelan island of Margarita, a popular getaway spot just a thirty-five-minute commercial flight from Maiquetia Airport on the country's mainland, I began to look for another job, one hopefully closer to the Santa Ines section, where we lived. Fortunately, I discovered that internationally known Berlitz Language School wanted to hire new English-speaking instructors at their headquarters building in an area in the city an easy walk from the apartment. Upon my arrival, a staff member greeted me warmly and enthusiastically. I explained that even though I hadn't taught a language before, I had prior instructional experience in teaching tennis in several facilities as well as previous employment as a substitute teacher in Massachusetts public schools. That must have been enough for me to be quickly hired. Within days I was being trained along with about a half dozen other men and women, to teach English to individuals and groups.

Training followed the specific method of instruction unique to Berlitz schools. I quickly became very familiar with the Spanish phrase, "Repita, por favor," which in English means "Repeat, please." The Berlitz method requires the student to repeat words out loud, so the instructor constantly asks that person to repeat back what was

During my Berlitz School stint, I usually worked at the headquarters in the Las Mercedes section of Caracas.

On some occasions during my Berlitz School stint, I went to the branch school on Avenida Urdeneta in downtown Caracas.

said to him or her. I said that phrase so often in both training sessions and later in my classes that I am surprised I didn't wake up in the middle of the night insisting to my imaginary student, "Repita, por favor."

Of course, the Berlitz method of language instruction also involves lively verbal interaction between the teacher and the student. I had little room for ad-libbing in class. Berlitz requires the teacher to follow each day's lesson plan strictly, according to the Berlitz instruction manual given to each instructor. A supervisor regularly monitored classes to be certain we followed the lesson plans. I never enjoyed being monitored, but generally supervisors gave me positive and encouraging reviews.

One of my more memorable students was a famous young actor, Franklin Virgues, on a popular daytime Venezuelan television soap opera. I found him a very likeable guy, and he fit in well with the rest of the students in the class. And then I taught some little rich kids driven to the school in chauffeured limousines. Enough said.

Over time, my supervisor asked me to teach in two Berlitz branch locations in Caracas, one downtown and the other in a section called La Urbina. I therefore got the opportunity to see areas of Caracas I had not visited before. When I traveled to the branch offices, I often used my lunch hour to familiarize myself with that area of the city as well as grab a quick bite from one of the local food trucks patronized by the native Caraqueños.

Of course, I could not call all days with Berlitz satisfying and fun. One day that I recall with anger and frustration, my supervisor scheduled me to teach a class at the school's downtown location and then also scheduled me to teach a class way back at the headquarters building in Las Mercedes just a few minutes after the conclusion of my first class. When I saw the schedule, I immediately realized I could not possibly get from downtown to headquarters in the short time allowed. I didn't have use of a car at the time, and consequently I would have to rely on the unfamiliar public transportation or cover the entire distance by foot regardless of the weather. Neither provided a good option for me, but, in my opinion, those were my only two choices.

I always liked to buy food from food trucks, like this one in La Urbina where I often bought a hot lunch.

You may be thinking, well, why didn't you just take a taxi? It all came down to finances. I figured if I paid for a taxi to take me to headquarters from my downtown class, the cost of that taxi ride would equal my pay for teaching the next couple of classes. That seemed like a foolish thing to do.

I told my supervisor I needed more time between the two classes in order to be on time for the second one. For some unknown reason, the supervisor didn't see the reason for my concern, and he refused to revise my schedule.

Well, when that day came, as soon as my class downtown ended, I left the building and started walking as fast as I could on what I thought the quickest route to get to headquarters. It was a hot, muggy day, and I quickly began to sweat, but I felt determined to get to my next class on time. I might have done it if I knew that area well, but somehow, somewhere I got myself turned around. I found myself at the end of a dead-end street I did not recognize.

I had never been in many sections of Caracas, and to my great frustration, the dead-end street apparently was one of them. Anyway, I will spare you any more details of my desperate and miserable hike and share with you that I did eventually get to the school in Las Mercedes. However, not only did I arrive about ten minutes late to start the class, but I arrived in terrible shape. My clothes were drenched in sweat and totally disheveled, and judging by the looks I received from my students as I entered the classroom, I must have spooked them pretty badly. I felt furious with my supervisor for putting me in that impossible and humiliating situation, and I made sure that it did not happen again.

Now that I have complained about a particularly bad day while I worked at Berlitz Language School in Caracas, please allow me to crow a little about a particularly great assignment, one that I agreed to without hesitation. The then foreign minister of Venezuela, Jose Alberto Zambrano-Velasco, had asked Berlitz Language School to provide him an English-speaking American once a week to help him improve his English proficiency. The classes would take place at his government office in the lovely and historically significant Casa Amarilla building, traditional home of the country's ministry of foreign affairs. I was thrilled to accept that assignment and looked forward to my first class with the foreign minister.

I wanted not only to meet him but also to observe how things operated at such a high level of the Venezuelan government. When I arrived at Casa Amarilla for the first class, a pair of security guards met me at the side entrance of the impressive

The Venezuelan Foreign Minister, Señor Alberto Zambrano-Velasco, had me read articles to him in English from Time *magazine.*

building. Before they allowed me in, they made necessary calls to the foreign minister's office to be sure I was scheduled to be teaching the honorable Senòr Zambrano-Velasco that day. Once inside, another government official escorted me up a flight of several stairs and into a long hallway that overlooked the floor below.

I walked past even more security personnel before eventually reaching the spacious ministry of foreign affairs' reception area. There the foreign minister's secretary told me that Señor Zambrano-Velasco expected me and would meet with me shortly. Within minutes, he came to the door, greeted me warmly, and speaking to me in very acceptable English, welcomed me into his large office.

After exchanging pleasantries, the foreign minister explained that, while he spoke passable English and understood it fairly well, he had contacted Berlitz because he wanted to increase his English skills. To my surprise and amazement, he then handed

The Venezuelan Foreign Minister had me read articles to him in English from an edition Time *magazine headlined* Mexico's Crisis

me a current English version of Time magazine and asked me to read it to him. And that is what I proceeded to do for the rest of the hour-long instruction period.

He wanted to hear how a true gringo speaks English. He had decided on the *Time* magazine method to increase his ability to communicate in my native language by hearing me or someone like me read and speak it. I had a little difficulty fulfilling my assignment, because the speaking blocks I mentioned earlier during my Vietnam reminiscence sometimes interrupted my reading out loud to him. He didn't seem to care about that, however, and the first lesson seemed to zoom by.

During the lesson, I marveled at the government setting I found myself in. I tried to steal a few glances around the room in order to absorb as much information about his office and its furnishings as I could. At some point in that first class, the foreign minister made a point of showing me a framed, autographed picture of US General Alexander Haig prominently displayed on his wall. As I recall, the personal inscription on the photograph read "To my dear friend, Jose Alberto . . . Al." Obviously, he was very proud of his relationship with General Haig.

I also became very aware of frequent clackety clack sounds made by the room's large teletype machine as it sent and received official and sometimes sensitive messages for the ministry. At the conclusion of class, I made sure that the Foreign Minister wanted to continue with the instruction for the next several weeks. When he replied in the affirmative, I asked if he would be kind enough to issue me some kind of written authorization enabling me to quickly pass through the series of security stations the next time I arrived.

Within minutes, Señor Zambrano-Velasco's personal secretary provided me with the document, and I pretty much floated out of Casa Amarilla's door a short time later. I was very excited about meeting and tutoring Venezuela's Foreign Minister, the chance to see in-real time how his ministry operated, and issuance to me of an official government pass allowing me smooth access to the foreign minister's reception area for the weekly allotted time.

Remember when I previously mentioned the surreal feeling that I experienced at my Sheraton

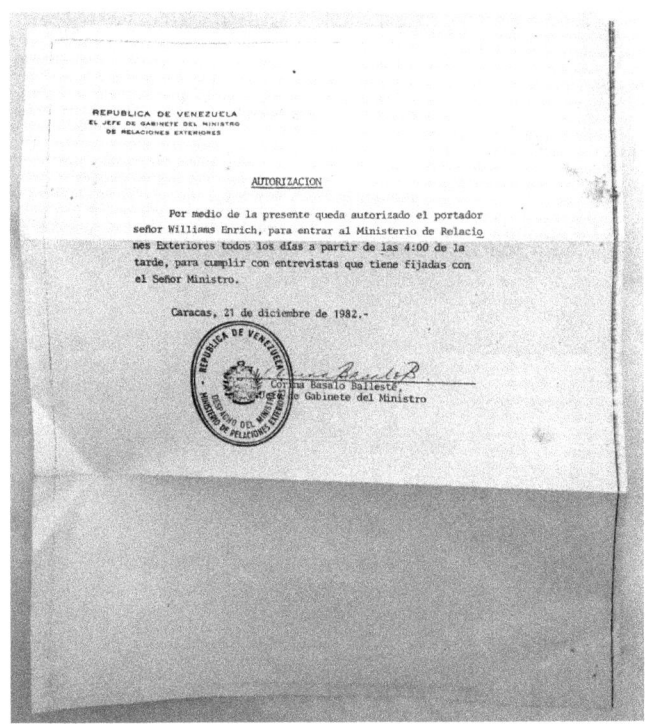

I had official authorization for admission to the office of the foreign minister in Venezuela during my employment with the Berlitz School.

Hotel buddy's wedding ceremony a few months earlier? Well, tutoring the Venezuelan foreign minister also made for a surreal experience. If you had told me that I would be sitting in the office of the Venezuelan foreign minister while reading an English edition of *Time* magazine out loud to the distinguished diplomat himself, I would have thought you were, as they say in Spanish, loco.

In the weeks that followed, my English-language instruction with the Foreign Minister always followed the same general pattern with him listening intently to me as I read out loud to him. And the issuance to me of the official pass by his office proved to be as helpful as I thought it would be for entering and exiting his building. Upon leaving Casa Amarilla, I entered neighboring Plaza Bolivar, a site of great historical significance to Venezuelans.

Plaza Bolivar takes its name from legendary Simon Bolivar who led the fight for Venezuela's independence from Spain. History books mention a balcony of Casa Amarilla as the setting for a brave vote of no confidence from citizens gathered in the plaza as to Spain continuing to rule the country. With that clear expression of decisive popular sentiment, the revolution for independence began.

Pigeons, other animals, and people crowd Plaza Bolivar in Caracas in front of Casa Amarilla, the site of the Venezuelan Foreign Ministry.

    Well-maintained tropical plants of all kinds grew alongside traditional walkways throughout the open and welcoming space. If you were lucky, as you strolled through the plaza, you would be treated to the sight of a sloth, an animal more associated with the Amazon jungle than an urban plaza. When I spotted it, it appeared surprisingly comfortable with its surroundings as it moved slowly but steadily through the walkways and greenery of the famous square. And I enjoyed not only observing the sloth but also a two-foot-long iguana that also appeared to be a resident of the plaza. The native populace appeared to fully accept and admire both animals.

Once I had established myself at Berlitz Language School as a full-time English instructor, I felt secure and comfortable enough to experience more of the sights and sounds of Caracas in earnest. I heard music played and enjoyed everywhere in the city. Most of the city's bus and taxi drivers had their vehicles' radio speakers blasting out their favorite salsa rhythms to themselves and their customers. Usually they cranked the volume so loud that the music easily reached the ears of anyone in the vicinity of those vehicles.

Along with frequent sounds of squealing brakes and honking horns on crowded streets, the powerful Latin beats made for a unique combination of sounds continually serenading the city dweller. Except for salsa music, my wife, parents-in-law, and I heard those sounds of screeching brakes, blaring car horns, and often car crashes pretty much every night from our high-rise apartment. I can't recall a single night during my stay when that cacophony of irritating and jarring sounds didn't reach into our apartment from the highway below. But somehow, all of those nightly assaults on our auditory nerves became just a part of usual background noise we had grown accustomed to, so unless a severe accident occurred or unusually loud shouts and insults emanated from drivers below, life went on as usual.

Constant music throughout the city's environs provided a backdrop for an incredible number of bars, nightclubs, and restaurants that catered to every resident and visitor's whim and pleasure. You could find every imaginable cuisine in Caracas. Patrons packed those eating establishments deep into the night as evidenced by habits of the typical Venezuelan frequenting a favorite bar or restaurant until early morning hours.

I thoroughly enjoyed eating and drinking at a good quality restaurant there. My favorite was Kanavayen Prado, a wonderful place in Caracas where you could eat, drink, and relax for hours at a time. It served the finest food and often offered delightful musical arrangements from an expert piano player situated near the dining tables. In fact, my well-known father-in-law, Anibal, sometimes was asked to play that same piano as a special treat for Kanavayen diners. The piano had

Kanavayen Prado was my favorite restaurant in Caracas.

originally belonged to my wife, who played it during her youth in her home. When she no longer wanted it, her father sold it to the restaurant.

At Kanavayen, I especially appreciated that I never felt hurried by the bartender or servers. After we finished the main dining course there, we often enjoyed an additional round of drinks, an extended period of sampling of desserts, or just pleasant conversation and socializing that could last for an extra hour or two. Compare that with the frustrated and angry looks you often get from staff at eating establishments in the United States if you continue to sit and socialize with your partner a few minutes beyond the completion of your meal. Then it is easy to conclude that management just wants to get you out of that seat as fast as possible after you have paid the bill so that they can quickly fill that table again with new paying customers. I think that you will agree, that kind of attitude from the staff of a dining establishment is just not conducive to a satisfactory and pleasant experience with friends or family. In my opinion, the traditional Venezuelan dining experience is absolutely the way to go.

That patron-friendly attitude can also be said to exist for traditional Caracas bars, and probably even more so in similar establishments in smaller Venezuelan towns and villages. One day, a very small and unassuming drinking establishment captivated me immediately as I walked along the city streets. When I entered, I felt as if it had all the aspects of a perfect neighborhood bar.

I ordered a bottle of Polar, an extremely popular beer brewed and produced in Venezuela, and let myself enjoy the atmosphere. After a while, since it wasn't busy, the bartender walked over to a small table occupied toward the back by a woman who appeared to be a good, if not intimate, friend of his, and joined her in almost whispered conversation. The bar wasn't lit very well, and the two of them sat in an area of even less light.

The setting and atmosphere of that bar made me think of a scene from a Humphrey Bogart/Lauren Bacall movie. The bartender, during a slow period at his small establishment, joining his girlfriend or at the very least a woman whom he obviously hoped to be his girlfriend in the future, at that dimly lit table towards the back; the American guy, namely me, sitting at the bar along with what appeared to be a couple of regular patrons from the neighborhood; the faded appearance of the walls; a few unoccupied tables in the room; all contributed to what was to me an iconic bar scene. I'll say it again. It was absolutely perfect.

I wouldn't change a thing.

My wife and I lived with her parents in their apartment in a high-rise building in Caracas.

A live musical performance on the stage of the Hilton Hotel by the renowned Spanish singer Raphael provided another inimitable experience for me in Caracas. Even though I did not know about his fame and popularity in Europe and South America, his singing instantly attracted me one day on a shopping excursion with my wife.

I happened to pass by a shop selling a variety of items and heard one of Raphael's most popular songs, I think "En Carne Vida," emanating from a small TV in the shop. The singer and song captivated me, and I began to take an active interest in Raphael's recordings.

We often relaxed in the living room in my in-laws' Caracas apartment.

Soon after, I told my mother-in-law, Gisela, of my new-found enthusiasm for the Spanish singer, and, God bless her, without my knowledge, she began to try to find a venue where I could see him in-person. Just a few weeks later, Gisela, told me she had learned that Raphael would soon perform in Caracas as part of a South American concert tour. With a smile, she asked if I would like to attend one of those live performances. She knew what my response would be, and the event turned out an even better musical experience than I had hoped.

My wife, my mother-in-law, and I went to the Hilton the night of the concert where we had very good seats not far from the stage. The minute the curtains parted and Raphael appeared, the singer immediately drew me in with his proud, regal bearing and superb artistic quality of his presentation as he sang many of his popular musical recordings. After a particularly spectacular rendering of one of his songs, I found myself giving him a standing ovation. I hadn't even thought about it. I just found myself standing and wildly cheering this incredibly talented singer.

I wish you had been there with us to thrill in the performance by a true artist in his craft. Little did I know that years later I would have the pleasure of shaking Raphael's hand and welcoming him to the United States. I attended one of his concerts in

My mother-in-law, Gisela, left, and my wife, Silvia, had a close relationship.

Tampa and received a pass to a meet-the-artist event immediately following his concert appearance. I never thought I would have a chance to meet the unforgettable Raphael in person, and it was a distinct thrill and memorable experience.

Please also allow me to tell you about an exciting experience I had within the field of social work during my stay in Venezuela. One of my wife's aunts had worked as a social worker for years in Caracas. Every Thursday evening, my wife and I dined with the aunt, her husband, and other family members at their apartment in Mariperez. When she learned of my education and employment in her field in the United States, she graciously contacted a friend, the director of a mental health hospital, to see if I might have an opportunity to further my social work experience. She arranged an interview for me with the gentlemen, and after I met with him for a few minutes in his office, he asked me if I would be agreeable to doing a presentation before his staff of mental health workers.

I explained that I had but a rudimentary command of Spanish but said I would be happy to do the presentation. We agreed on a date for the event. Upon returning to the apartment, I wrote up a general description of subjects studied in order to obtain a master's degree in social work in US colleges as well as required field work in outside agencies. My wife translated my written words into Spanish. I ran through my prepared talk with Silvia in Spanish a couple of times to be ready for my presentation.

Just a few days later I found myself standing on a small stage with the facility director as I faced twenty-five or so people in attendance. Although I felt nervous at first and shaky at the beginning of my talk, I completed it satisfactorily. The next part of the event proved a lot more difficult for me because I had to field questions from members of the audience in Spanish, and I didn't understand much of the content addressed to me. Fortunately, the director kindly jumped in and served as my impromptu translator, so I could answer questions.

Overall, the presentation was a success. When I met with the director again a week later, it soon became apparent, however, that he and I came from different directions as far as my possible continued participation in his program. He wanted me to involve myself strictly with employee education, whereas I hoped to work directly with patients. Due to that disappointing impasse, the director and I had no more contact. I did, however, save the sign put up in the facility's hallway announcing my upcoming social work presentation and inviting all employees to attend. It still serves as a nice reminder of another totally new experience I had while living in that South American country.

Manny Trillo is at bat at a Winter League baseball game in Caracas.

I would like to share some of my experiences in the world of sports in Venezuela. First of all, it surprised me to learn that baseball was more popular than soccer. I always associated South America with soccer, or futbol as they call it there. Of course, people played soccer, but not with the enthusiasm and passion that baseball brought out in Venezuelans. Throughout the country, young men of all ages played baseball, and the country supported a highly regarded professional baseball league, known in the US as the Winter League. It included not only major leaguers who wanted to hone their skills during the off-season, but also native Venezuelans of such a high level of skill or promise that several ended up playing on major league US teams.

Silvia's Cousin Freddie showed me the workings of the arena in Maracay.

Another sporting event older than soccer or baseball and famous for tradition and pageantry takes place in Venezuela. Yes, you got my drift. Bullfighting. A cruel tradition, to be sure, it inflicts much pain on the bull and often ends in its death. But I heard enough about the tradition that it intrigued me. When I had an opportunity to attend a bullfight near Caracas, I admit that I jumped at the chance. During my stay in Venezuela, I attended three bullfights, one in Caracas, one in the nearby city of Maracay, and the third in Valencia. Bullfights traditionally take place in Plazas Monumentales.

One of my wife's cousins made a business of transporting bulls from ranches in Mexico to bullfighting arenas in Venezuela. He kindly enhanced my experience as a spectator and my education in the business end of bullfighting when he met me one day at the Caracas arena. He led me on a tour of interior rooms, pens, and passageways of the imposing concrete building. He showed me separate pens for bulls under the arena's seats before an event begins. At the right time, a handler coaxes them toward the sturdy door opening into the ring.

Before the bullfight began that same day, Silvia and I watched from concrete seats as the traditional pageantry unfolded. Men on horseback sounded bugles to announce the entry of other horseback riders and attendants who would assist in the ring. Then, to the roar of the crowd, the matador himself appeared. Most everyone in the ring wore traditional and quite colorful bullfighting attire. They waited attentively, some on horseback and some on foot, to assist from their first sight of the bull in the ring in the event of the bull threatening to gore the matador. Heavy padding on both sides of the horses' imposing bodies protects them if an angry bull charges the horse and its rider with its dangerous horns.

Bull versus matador: as you know, not always does the matador win. However, in matchups between bull and matador we saw that day, the bull lost its life in all of them.

I don't know the intricacies of bullfighting tradition, but suffice it to say that, by deftly handling his red cape, the matador provokes the bull to charge. When the bull does charge, the matador skillfully allows the powerful animal to get just close enough to allow the man to plunge sharp lances into the bull's thick hide. That, in turn, causes the bull pain and blood loss, and consequently, the animal grows even more infuriated.

With bloody lances dangling from its side, the enraged bull eventually charges the red cloth again. Then the matador delivers a final and fatal blow by plunging a larger, more lethal lance into the wounded animal. If the matador strikes the bull in the right location, the animal dies within seconds. Once the bull dies, men called muleteros immediately drag the bull out of the ring on a mat.

Silvia waits for a bullfight to start. I needed this ticket for admission to the bullfight at Nuevo Circo on June 6, 1982.

*The crowd enters the bullfight arena at Maracay, top.
A bullfight begins in Maracay, above.*

The bull charges a horseback rider in the Maracay arena, top. Muleteers drag a dead bull from the Maracay arena, above.

It sounds brutal. It is brutal. But bullfighting remains a popular tradition and entertainment for many residents of Venezuela and other South American countries.

I couldn't describe my experience of Caracas without mentioning a form of transportation that fascinated me, namely the city's minivans and cars, in Spanish, por puestos. An inexpensive and popular way to get around the city, those small vans seemed to be everywhere. Along with the usual colorful and extroverted driver at the wheel, the minivans hold a maximum of six passengers and the cars, up to five. They follow regular, prescribed routes throughout Caracas. The word puesto in Spanish means seat, so por puesto means the passenger pays for a seat in the vehicle.

When I was there, if you didn't want to wait for a taxi or did want to save some money, por puestos were the way to go. Once you got into the minivan or car, you paid the driver a standard fare, and quickly looked around to find a seat in the usually crowded vehicle. When you approached your desired stop, you yelled out "Por aqui, por favor," which means "right here, if you please." The driver would then stop the vehicle and let you exit.

Sounds easy, doesn't it? Well, in most of my experiences using those minivans or cars, it was. However, sometimes I found myself wedged in that small interior space with a group of people engaged in loud and animated conversation, and the driver's radio blaring out the latest salsa hit. Believe me, that situation required a firm, persistent voice to get the driver's attention. It was simply all part of living in a different and sometimes frustrating South American culture.

In the following personal tale of por puesto woe, it wasn't Venezuelan culture that frustrated me. No, it was me that frustrated me and left me stranded in an unknown and unwanted location somewhere on the streets of Caracas.

What happened to me that day began innocently enough. I waved down a por puesto, quickly jumped inside, then squeezed into one of the minivan's seats. A few minutes later, as we approached the area where I wanted to get off, the loud voices and music in the crowded vehicle made me feel anxious about my ability to get my voice heard by the driver. And when I get nervous, as I mentioned earlier, I often block on words and can't verbalize them.

That's exactly what happened. As hard as I tried and as much as I wanted to, when it came time to yell out the "por aqui, por favor," I simply could not say the words. And since there is no other way in a por puesto for a passenger to communicate with the driver, the driver of course drove right by my stop and continued down the long highway. Caught in that confounding situation, I wound up having to wait until the very end of the scheduled route before I could exit the vehicle.

Do you think owners of the por puestos would ever install hanging ropes they have above windows in many public buses in the States? The ones that you can pull to alert the driver you want to be let out at the next stop? If they ever do, and I'm ever back in Venezuela, I'll be a lot more frequent and relaxed passenger.

As promised, let me talk about (I should say scream about, but I'll be nice) what fell under the category of postal system in Venezuela back in the 1980s. It would be comical if it weren't so irritatingly incomprehensible. Take, for example, what it took for me to mail a letter at the main post office building in the heart of Caracas. Since I didn't know the monetary value of the stamp I needed to send my letter overseas, I found myself standing for quite a while in a long line until I reached the person behind the counter. Thinking that the postal employee in front of me would accomplish the necessary tasks to enable me to send my letter, I was astonished to discover that all she did was to weigh my envelope with the letter inside, carefully write on my envelope what stamp was required, and hand the envelope back to me.

That's all she did. She then directed me to the end of another long line of people in that commodious room. Again, after several minutes of waiting to get to the head of the line, I couldn't believe what that employee did. After reading what the first employee had written on my envelope, she affixed the proper stamp and then handed the stamped envelope back to me. Incredibly, I needed a third postal clerk to complete the process. Yes, by that time I felt like screaming, because, my God, standing in three long lines just to send one letter?? Unfortunately, the answer was yes, and there was no getting around the system.

When at last I got to the head of the third line that morning, I handed the stamped envelope to still another postal employee whose sole job involved date-stamping my envelope and accepting it for dispatch. I cannot imagine the unfathomable process my envelope took from that point on to reach the United States. In fact, I cannot imagine what steps it went through just to get out of that postal building. It could have taken weeks, for all I know.

I do know that one time I purchased a few postcards at the Maiquetia International Airport while waiting for a flight back to the States. Once I completed my helloes and addresses on the cards after placing the proper stamps on them, I looked without success in the airport for a mailbox. When the employee at the small shop where I had bought the postcards heard that I couldn't find a mailbox, she offered to send them for me along with several other people's letters and cards. Astonishingly, I had been back in the United States more than three months before those postcards arrived at their proper destinations.

I also experienced the distinct pleasure (not) of trying to obtain an official identification card, known in Venezuela as a cedula, from the government. Along with a passport, it identified a person in good standing in that country. A government agency in Caracas issued the photo IDs, so one morning I stood in a long line to do whatever I had to do to obtain my card. The line moved very slowly in the morning heat, but eventually I reached the counter where I had to fill out an application and be ready to have a photograph taken.

So far, despite the time that I had spent waiting in line, things seemed to move along so well that I began to dismiss the warnings I had received from some members of my Venezuelan family. They said the process could be long and difficult for me as a foreigner.

Having filled out the application form and handed it back to the clerk behind the counter, I sat and waited with other applicants for another couple of hours before the officials called my name. They told me to sit in front of a blank screen and look directly at a camera for several seconds. Once that was done, they told me I had completed my application process. They said I should return to the agency in a week in order to pick up my cedula.

Pleased with myself that I had successfully navigated the agency's bureaucratic procedures, I announced when I got back to the apartment that I hadn't really found it that tough to do. Right then, I should have realized the warnings I had received about the application process and especially for gringos came from citizens with years and years of frustrating and unpleasant experience in dealing with governmental bureaucracies.

It didn't seem to matter which person or political party held office at the time. The service provided by the government worker usually verged on deplorable. The steps an applicant had to take in order to obtain whatever official documentation he or she sought often qualified as exasperating and sometimes inexplicable.

As for my pursuit of a photo identification card, all of the warnings turned out to be true. Of course, my family members had it right all along. When the following week rolled around, I respectfully got at the end of the long line at the government building and waited to move to the front where I could presumably pick up my official ID.

When I reached the agency's front counter, I gave my name and told the clerk that I wanted to pick up my cedula. She, in turn, checked some records and informed me to come back next week because the agency hadn't completed my ID. And now, you undoubtedly know what I am going to say next and again and again and yes, even again. One day each week, for the next several weeks, stubbornly sticking to my belief that the system would finally work for me, I took my place in line. But, of course, my application did not constitute the exception to the rule, and upon my reaching the front counter and meeting with the clerk, I always heard the same thing: "Your cedula isn't ready yet. Come back in one week."

After more than two months of that nonsense, I promised myself that next time I would find out the problem even if it meant that I had to pay an "extra fee." Okay, yes, a bribe. When I got to the front of the line that morning, I somehow got lucky and caught the attention of one of the other employees in the office. That woman actually helped, and soon I learned the reason for my long frustrating wait was that I had blinked when they took my picture during my first visit and my picture was therefore deemed unacceptable.

I had stood in line one day every week for two months and then they told me that they delayed completion of my application because my photo didn't pass the blink test?? They couldn't have taken another picture at the same time?? I was in such a state of disbelief that I don't honestly remember having a second photograph taken, but let me save you the unpleasantness of listening to any more whining from me and inform you that eventually in my first year in Venezuela, I did manage to get Cedula #81.528.867. The important universal lesson I learned? Listen carefully when an experienced person gives you advice.

It took quite some time, but eventually I got my Venezuelan ID card.

123

Have you ever heard of the island of Margarita? Back in the United States, whenever people talked about the many island paradises of the Caribbean, they did not include Margarita. Maybe the Venezuelan government did not do a good job of promoting Margarita as an international destination or maybe it is too far from the US. Still, its pristine beaches, intriguing coastal fishing villages, and friendly people deserve mention.

Margarita is located just off the Venezuelan mainland near the coastal towns of Rio Chico and Puerto La Cruz. Puerto La Cruz offered a two-hour ferry ride to the appealing island that stretches forty-eight miles in length and twelve miles in width. Its tumultuous human history dates back many hundreds of years. Several times, ruthless pirates raided and occupied it, and sometimes so did brutal Spanish conquistadors for the island's gold and natural pearls.

Old Spanish forts still dot the island, and along with the more than fifty magnificent beaches that ring Margarita, those impressive fortifications became tourist attractions for those from the Venezuelan mainland who wanted to get away from big-city living for a long weekend or maybe for a one- or two-week vacation.

Years ago, my wife's parents purchased a small apartment convenient to downtown Porlamar, the island's most populated city, and it was there that my wife, her parents, and I stayed on at least two occasions for a few days and nights. We rented a Volkswagen Bug at the Margarita Airport and explored the island.

One time, we visited a relatively secluded area known as La Laguna de la Restinga and famous for the fine pearls harvested from its healthy, innumerable oyster beds. There, you could purchase exquisite pearls of worldwide renown for very reasonable prices.

Natives of the island even sold those valuable gems, most commonly of white or bluish-grey color, on many of the beautiful beaches of Margarita. They often approached us as we relaxed on the sand holding two or three of the island's precious pearls wrapped in cloth. Because a small wooden bridge separates the oyster-rich area of Margarita from where the average tourist visited when we were there, I felt as if we had taken a step back in time to a more authentic representation of the island and its people.

I took one of my favorite photographs there when we stopped at a nearby beach to take in the scene with its fresh air and saltwater ambiance. An elderly woman from the local coastal village happened to be walking along the beach, and with small colorful village fishing boats in the background, it seemed a magical photographic opportunity.

A resident walks the beach on the southern end of Margarita.

Another time on Margarita, we drove our rented VW Bug out of Porlamar and into the much less populated interior of the island. We drove past makeshift little shacks along the roadside where entire families resided, along with some chickens and a pig or two. The arid soil looked dry, infertile, and extremely difficult for a family to farm either plants or animals in that unforgiving environment without good access to water. In many cases, it appeared the lack of available fresh water made it next to impossible for a farming family to break out of their subsistence lifestyle and extreme poverty.

Desert claimed much of the island and, as a result, made home to several varieties of cactus plants. It also hosted semi-wild burros that appeared to have free rein of the many open hills and mountains. I recall one day we drove to the top of a big hill overlooking the Caribbean Sea and came upon a burro just taking it easy in the intense heat and seemingly oblivious to us and our small automobile. That sandy and dusty landscape with its many cacti and occasional grazing burros contrasted sharply with the bustling little capital of Pampatar just a few miles away.

I fell in love with the remote, little fishing villages that accompanied many beautiful natural island harbors, especially the magical communities of Pedro Gonzalez and of Juan Griego. Small homes, some of concrete blocks and others of far less durable material, sat just a few feet from the high water mark of the sea. Each sported a separate, usually pastel, color for row upon row of perhaps a dozen tiny homes, one

An old Spanish fort on the island of Margarita dwarfs my wife, Silvia.

Margarita homes shared traditional architectural features in the 1970s, and fishing boats lined up near a Margarita coastal village.

I spent a moment in the sun at Pedro Gonzalez Beach on Margarita, top, while Silvia sunbathed near our rented Volkswagen on Margarita, above.

I sat on the sea wall at Pedro Gonzales, Margarita, with Silvia, Silvia's cousin Lizbeth, and her Canadian friend, Kevin.

*We liked to swim at Pedro Gonzales Beach on Margarita, top.
The little fishing village of Pedro Gonzales spread along the beach, above.*

painted light blue, one painted light green, one painted light yellow, and on and on as they formed a colorful line facing the sandy beach.

Small imaginatively colored wooden fishing boats lay scattered along the shoreline until their owners took them from shore to catch fish. The painted and traditional fishermen's homes, colorful and traditional wooden fishing boats, cactus-filled hills in the background, and, in the foreground, a natural, sandy beach welcoming the waters of the Caribbean Sea composed a photographer's dream. I took photo after photo of the magnificent scenes.

To my astonishment, one coastal town, seemingly located in the middle of nowhere, housed a small military detachment. I could not imagine why the government felt a tiny military installation necessary in that far off fishing village. Looking back on my days in the war zone of South Vietnam, I would have paid a mighty ransom for assignment to that military detachment on the island of Margarita for my entire tour of duty. There couldn't have been more than four or five members of the military assigned to that beachside outpost, and it certainly didn't appear that the neighboring village needed to be protected from outside antagonists in any way.

But what did this gringo know? Perhaps a perfectly good reason placed the detachment there, or maybe not. It didn't matter. In true Venezuelan fashion, being stationed there was reason enough to be there.

Now, I must be losing it a bit, because I somehow neglected to tell you about one of the most important destinations for travelers fortunate enough to visit the wonderful fishing villages by the sea. Most of them included a shack, and I mean shack, that advertised "cerveza, bien fria" along with ever-present bottles of Coca-Cola. Yes, those wonderful little shacks offered ice-cold Polar beer, the Venezuelan beverage of choice, and when you came off the beach all hot and sweaty, nothing satisfied the thirst buds better than a cold bottle of beer pulled from an old, leaky freezer filled to the top with ice.

Traditionally, that old freezer always sported a faded Coca-Cola decal on its side and took up most of the shack's space. Trust me on this: If you ever find yourself in Venezuela and the scenario prevails, you gotta experience it. It is not just the ice-cold beer. Well, to be honest, a lot of it is, but . . . The point is the traditional Venezuelan setting where you down that beer is a scenario way over the top. The experience resembles that old beer advertisement on TV when the beer-drinkers agree: "It doesn't get any better than this."

Enough said. Have one on me, and enjoy.

We had a fine view of the residence below our apartment in Porlamar, Margarita.

Personally, I loved the tiny apartment owned by my parents-in-law where we stayed while visiting Margarita. Not luxurious but perfectly functional, it featured a balcony looking out over a less developed area of the island. We could see one or two construction sites from the balcony, although they were far enough away from our building so as not to disrupt the peace and quiet of our tiny hideaway.

We always delighted in hearing the crowing of a full-throated rooster each morning. The sound came from a native family's residence way below our balcony. If you looked down from that balcony, you also caught a glimpse of one or two of that family's large pigs as they roamed their property looking for scraps of food.

Whenever I stayed in that small apartment, I looked forward to hearing the rooster crow in the morning and to seeing family members attending to their animals' needs.

I also enjoyed exploring the unique downtown section of Porlamar, but only after I secured the heavy, barred front metal door common to all entrances on the island as well as in the major cities of Venezuela. A popular open-air market fascinated me most as I explored. It sold practically anything you could think of in terms of food, clothing, furnishings, and small appliances. I loved seeing the huge variety of items for sale as well as shoppers walking the aisles looking for bargains.

If you really wanted to get off-the-beaten-track on the island and you had the luxury of owning or renting a four-wheel drive vehicle like a Land Rover or Jeep, you could have entire spectacular beaches to yourself. Steep and sometimes treacherous trails through remote hills of sand, cactus, and the occasional burro eventually led down to the open sea, and many of the trails brought the driver and his lucky passengers to pristine beaches and harbors that could only be reached that way or by boat. I never did have the pleasure of visiting those hidden coves of sand and waves, but if I had a bucket list, that experience would be on it.

Fishing boats moored in the Pedro Gonzales harbor of Margarita.

To thank the Blessed Virgin for answering prayers, pilgrims often made their way to La Virgen del Valle Basilica on the island of Margarita.

Supplicants approached the altar of the Blessed Virgin in La Virgen del Valle Basilica with pleas and thanks.

The people who lived in those fishing villages generation after generation appeared to be happy and healthy, despite their meager accumulations in terms of money and material possessions. Apparently, their way of life included a lot of beneficial things necessary for a happy and healthy existence such as a real sense of community, the importance of family, purposeful work in a natural setting, and probably a diet mainly consisting of fresh nutritious items directly from the sea.

Once, while exploring a part of one village, I came upon a goat napping at the foot of a gravestone in the local cemetery. Unfettered, the goat appeared to have the whole village as its home. It also had just given birth to a couple of baby goats right there at the cemetery.

Another time, I came upon a funeral procession headed to the cemetery. There wasn't an automobile in sight. Everybody in that procession of twenty or thirty village residents walked slowly together to honor deceased brethren. The simple, humble scene moved me, and taught me a lesson in respect, humility, and loyalty.

If you happened to look behind that group as I did, you would see an extremely large religious cross high atop one of the nearby mountains clearly visible to villagers below. I would hope that, as I write these words years later, the character and people of those small fishing villages nestled on the shores of the Caribbean Sea have not significantly changed since I visited them, but sadly, that is probably not the case. Better roads, better communication, and more tourists visiting the island would all contribute to inevitable cultural changes for those villagers. I am thankful that I could observe and experience some of what appeared to be more innocent times before progress came along to change the landscape and lifestyles of those native Venezuelans.

I must mention the Santuario de la Virgen del Valle located on Margarita's El Valle del Espiritu Santo. Venezuelan Catholics who make up the majority of Venezuelan Christians view the church as very special. For worshipers, here resides the patron saint Margarita, and especially in September of each year, true believers flock to the church for prayer, thanks, and renewal. My own mother-in-law, Gisela, made a promise to the Virgin Mary that if her daughter, my wife, Silvia, delivered a healthy baby, she would present the baby to the Virgin for answering her prayer. After our healthy baby, Stephanie, arrived in 1987, her grandmother knew she would make a visit of thanks with her to the Virgin Mary. Silvia, her father, and I had the privilege of joining her when she followed through on her promise at the church.

Choroni's magnificent beach attracts vacationers.

Silvia enjoyed wearing my old US Army shirt..

Next to the chapel, a museum housed many magnificent pearls donated by local fishermen when they presented them to the Virgin Mary as thank-yous for saving their lives at sea or for an abundant catch from the Caribbean.

And then there was Pepeganga, a popular variety store. Just the name of the store itself was fun.

If a visitor to the island wanted to enjoy genuine native food, one had only to drive along city streets until you came upon a person selling fresh empanadas stuffed with locally caught fish. Oh, empanadas taste delightful.

I can remember Silvia, her parents, and me pulling over in our rental car to buy freshly cooked empanadas from a street vendor. Those darned things tasted so delicious that a few minutes later we turned our VW around so we could visit that vendor again and enjoy a new batch of those mouth-watering treats.

Contrast that informal eating experience with the time we ate at a commercial restaurant across the street from our apartment building. After I ate what was advertised as a turkey dinner, I suffered terrible food poisoning for the next couple of days. In Venezuela, the street vendor offering freshly cooked and traditional foods can often be trusted more than the professional restaurants' offerings and for a lot less money.

My wife, my brother-in-law, and I took a trip to a magical place called Choroni during the Christmas holidays one year. What an adventure getting to the small coastal town. In order to reach Choroni by car (the other way is by boat), we had to take our life in our hands by driving up the side of a mountain, then across the mountain by way of a narrow and winding dirt road with very little space between our vehicle and steep cliffs overlooking valleys far below. It horrified me to think what would happen if one of the many commercial buses came barreling around the corner from the opposite direction.

Believe me, anyone who drove that mountain road would be an advocate for immediate installation of sturdy guardrails on all mountain roads. But it would not surprise me if several tragic accidents occurred every year on that perilous road. If I ever took a trip to Choroni again, yes, I would hope to find a way to get there by boat.

The three of us did somehow make it over that mountain in one piece and experienced the genuine pleasure of the remainder of the drive. We passed through a lovely national forest called Henri Pittier National Park on the way to the town, and then finally arrived at our destination.

In the colonial style, picture-perfect Choroni boasted streets swept clean, buildings well maintained, and no sign of graffiti or littering. With a population of

Tidy streets, swept clean daily, adorned Choroni.

Residents set up traditional Christmas decorations in the village of Choroni.

We saw a festive table in Choroni.

no more than five hundred, it appeared that the tiny municipality met the needs of all its residents.

I noticed a little police station across the street from the traditional plaza in the center of town. We entered a small store near the station to purchase some snacks. Then, to our amazement, after we asked where we could buy adult beverages, the man who sold us the snacks told us to go through a side door of the same store. The door opened into an adjacent tiny space where the very SAME man greeted us, this time offering to sell beer, Coca-Cola, and other bottled drinks. You got two stores for one at that location.

I relaxed in a hammock at a friend's home in Choroni.

Friends of our family had relatives who owned a house in Choroni. They invited us to spend the night and welcomed us with open arms. They offered each of us a relaxing rest in lovely and comfortable hammocks hanging in the home.

Since we arrived in the middle of the Christmas season, a crowd of revelers went from house to house to celebrate the baby Jesus's birth. Everyone who participated in the procession clearly enjoyed the celebration, and the large, happy group rejoiced in their Lord's birth into the wee hours of the night.

The following morning, Silvia, her brother, and I headed over to what had to be one of the most beautiful beaches in all of Venezuela. In order to get there, we had to cross a gently flowing stream on the outskirts of the town. I loved that no effort had been made to re-channel the water or otherwise change its direction to allow beachgoers easier access to the shore on the other side. Instead, it appeared that the stream and the residents of that town accepted each other as equals. The result made an ordinary walk or drive to the local beach a fun adventure.

We had a lovely host family in Choroni during the holidays.

I imagine water flowed down from nearby mountainsides because it was clear and cold. Once we cleared the stream, we continued down a dirt road until we came to an increasingly open area of palm trees and sand. Then the vista revealed as a slice of tropical paradise.

The white sandy beach stretched for maybe a half mile, and people of all ages swam or relaxed under coconut palms growing along fringes of the beach. A middle-aged woman expertly balanced a basket of freshly made empanadas on her head, a not uncommon sight along Venezuela's Caribbean beaches. I am sure that she did a fantastic business in that idyllic setting.

I walked to the far end of the beach and up a hill overlooking the incredibly beautiful scene. From that lofty perch, I could spot big schools of fish in the cove's azure waters because their density turned the surface water above them a dark color and those dark shapes in the water contrasted sharply with the transparent water around them. I heard later of another pristine beach on the other side of town, but I cannot imagine a more beautiful beach than the one we visited. It added to the overall allure of the area embracing the town of Choroni, its friendly residents, and its spectacular natural surroundings.

Another special place posed a strange fit for Venezuela, but it worked out well. People of German ancestry comprised the village of La Colonia Tovar. The immigrants from Germany came to Venezuela many years before through a mutual and amicable agreement between the two countries. They accomplished noteworthy things in their new land.

The group found a remote area high in the mountains and built traditional German homes and businesses, raised traditional German crops, and successfully transferred traditional German culture, including the German language, to their new home. Over many years, residents of La Colonia Tovar adapted from speaking German to fluency in Spanish. As a result, visitors from Caracas and surroundings began to make the long drive up the mountain to experience the town's unique way of life for a few relaxing days and nights. We did the same and found a fine, enjoyable setting while staying at the Selva Negra Hotel. For a treat there, I especially liked strawberries with cream famous in the German community. Cool, fresh air there made sleeping a pleasure in that mountaintop community.

Finally, I cannot leave out of this narrative my realization of the supreme importance of family in Venezuela. Family meant everything, and my wife's family provided a terrific example.

Silvia stood on the deck of our chalet in the Selva Negra Hotel in La Colonia Tovar, the German community. We sometimes swam in the pool with its fine view of the valley below at La Colonia Tovar.

From the time they first walk and talk, Venezuelan youngsters learn the supreme importance of family in their lives, and it stays with them forever. I often watched young children mingling comfortably and enjoyably with their elders, school-age cousins spending time at each other's homes to do their homework together, young family members enjoying sleepovers together, and on weekends attending parties together.

Every weekend, family members gathered for hours at a time at the grandmother's apartment in Caracas to eat, talk, and enjoy each other's company.

 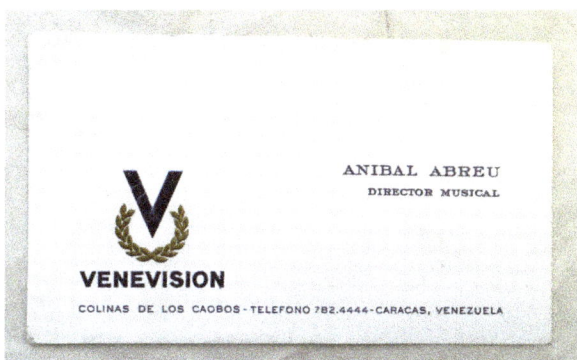

Silvia's dad, Anibal, was among founders of the Society of Writers and Composers of Venezuela. He served as president. Anibal worked for many years as the musical director of Venevision.

Everyone enjoyed the availability of food and drinks, and the inviting aroma Venezuelan foods added to the already welcoming atmosphere in the grandmother's or Mama Lola's home.

The family identified Mama Lola as the true matriarch. Imagine being the mother of ten children and, along with her hard-working husband, being tasked with the responsibility of bringing up so many children. Her children revered her for that achievement. They happily and faithfully gathered every weekend at her apartment to enjoy and honor her presence, a common Venezuelan experience repeated over and over again in thousands upon thousands of Venezuelan homes every week.

Tradition obligated surviving members of a deceased person's family to stay with

Gisela's mother, Mama Lola, left, and one of her daughters, Obu, helped me feel right at home in Venezuela.

the body until burial. Such a show of love and support made a big impression on me as I do not recall such an observance in my own family. Consequently, I considered it a great honor when one of my wife's relatives told me that she saw me just not as Silvia's husband but as a genuine member of the family. I will always treasure those words.

Are you wondering how *Have Racquet, Will Travel* remained a part of my life in Venezuela after I left my tennis pro position at the resort/hotel on the Caribbean? Yes, I worked for the rest of my time in Venezuela teaching the English language at Berlitz. However, a few months before I headed back to the United States, I briefly flirted with the idea of going back into teaching tennis after I saw an ad in a local English-language newspaper seeking an experienced tennis professional to join an already established enterprise in the Caracas area called Pro-Tenis.

I ended up talking on the phone with owner Mark Sydnor, and the available position sounded like a good opportunity for me. A short time later,

My father-in-law's mother, Carmen Rosa, paused in the kitchen, top. Silvia's brother, Hernan, took a phone call in my parents-in-laws' apartment.

Silvia, left, looked forward to birthday cake at her cousin's family swimming pool. Milagros and Raul waited to sing to her.

I met with him, and he asked me if I would assist with one of his scheduled lessons at a nearby tennis club. Even though I still experienced myself as a handicapped tennis professional because of my mental block when I had to hit a backhand shot, my assistance during Mark's tennis lesson must have gone reasonably well. On the drive back to my apartment, Mark asked me if I wanted to join his team of tennis instructors.

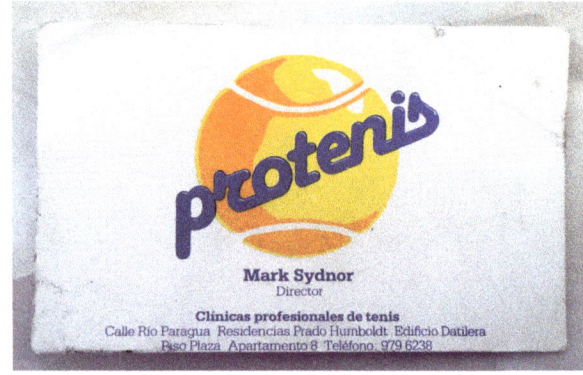

I saved Mark Sydnor's protenis *card.*

I expressed my interest, but because I didn't know how much longer I would stay in Venezuela, I didn't want to sign any work contract. I told Mark that my involvement needed to be day-to-day, and apparently he didn't want that in a new hire.

I didn't hear from him again after he dropped me off at my residence. My days of *Have Racquet, Will Travel* finally ended. Those special days spanned twenty important years of my life. Those years filled with experiences that I never would have envisioned when I received that wonderful wooden plaque way back as a teenager.

A tennis racquet, for me a significant talisman, and I traveled together for many years. I think that many of you will agree that it was a helluva trip together.

HAVE RACQUET · WILL TRAVEL

WIRE EMRICH
NEW ENGLAND
SOUTH VIETNAM · VENEZUELA

William Emrich

About the Author

Born in Norwalk, Connecticut, in 1947, William (Bill) Emrich didn't have to confront the more unforgiving and demanding aspects of daily living until after he graduated from Tufts University in 1969. Soon thereafter, a stint in the US Army in war-torn South Vietnam opened his eyes to many of life's realities. Upon his return to the States, the author struggled to "regain his footing" as he also tried to help others going through their own painful and private challenges as he obtained a masters degree and worked as a psychiatric social worker and later as a psychotherapist in greater Boston.

A veteran volunteer with the Pinellas County, Florida, Environmental Lands Division, Bill pursues life-long interest in the natural world that inspired him to complete the University of Florida Coastal Systems Module of the Florida Master Naturalist Program.

His column, "The Wildlife Side of Oldsmar," appeared in the Oldsmar, Florida, Community Newsletter for years. His photographs of nature have been exhibited in Florida and Maine.

Bill recently fulfilled his dream of buying lakeside property and having a cabin built overlooking that lake in the woods of coastal Maine. That experience both before and after the cabin's construction prompted him to write his first book, *Wild Maine Adventure*, published by Haley's in 2016.

Bill's career with the federal government transitioned in the late 1990s to civilian work with the Tampa, Florida, Police Department. He retired from the City of Tampa in 2009.

A US Army veteran of the 101st Airborne Division, Bill spent fourteen months in South Vietnam through April, 1971, where he earned a Bronze Star and an Army Commendation Medal. He was honorably discharged with the rank of sergeant.

Bill and his wife, Silvia Abreu of Caracas, Venezuela, have a daughter, Stephanie, who is a Clearwater, Florida, police officer, and a grandson, Anthony Stir.

Colophon

Text and captions for *Have Racquet • Will Travel* is set in Minion, a serif typeface designed by Robert Slimbach in 1990 for Adobe Systems and inspired by late Renaissance-era type. The name comes from the traditional naming system for type sizes, in which minion is between nonpareil and brevier, with the type body seven points in height As the name suggests, it is particularly intended as a font for body text in a classical style, neutral and practical while also slightly condensed to save space. Slimbach described the design as having "a simplified structure and moderate proportions."

Minion is a large family of fonts, including Greek and Cyrillic alphabets, optical sizes, condensed styles, and stylistic alternates such as swash capitals. It is one of the most popular typefaces used in books.

Titles for *Have Racquet • Will Travel* are set in Antique Olive, a humanist sans-serif typeface ("antique" being equivalent to sans-serif in French typographic conventions). Along the lines of Gill Sans, it was designed in the early 1960s by French typographer Roger Excoffon, an art director and former consultant to the Marseilles based Fonderie Olive. The key shapes, especially the letter O, resemble an olive, which is one of the characteristics which make Excoffon's typefaces unique.

Lewis Blackwell later commented on the design, "An attempt to offer a more refined sans serif than presented by Helvetica and Univers, but it was too characterful and too late to be widely adopted outside France."

www.ingramcontent.com/pod-product-compliance
Lightning Source LLC
Chambersburg PA
CBHW060939170426
43195CB00022B/2976